# MIDDLE MANAGEMENT IN THE PRIMARY SCHOOL

a development guide
for curriculum leaders,
subject managers and senior staff

## Second Edition

NEVILLE WEST

**David Fulton Publishers**
London

David Fulton Publishers Ltd
Ormond House, 26–27 Boswell Street, London WC1N 3JD

First published in Great Britain by David Fulton Publishers 1995
Second Edition 1998

British Library Cataloguing in Publication Data

A catalogue record for this book is available from the British Library

ISBN 1–85346–576–3

Typeset by FSH Print & Production Ltd, London
Printed in Great Britain by Hobbs the Printers Ltd, Totton, Hampshire

# Contents

# Dedication

This book is dedicated to the many scale-post holders, curriculum consultants and subject managers who have undertaken so much productive work in schools in the period since 1956, when middle management roles were first established in the primary sector.

# Preface to the Second Edition

The response to the first edition has proved very positive and the amendments to this new edition have been made in the light of feedback from providers who have used the book on development programmes for subject managers and from headteachers who have used it as a resource on school based development days. An evaluation of one of the lead programmes was carried out by The International School Effectiveness and Improvement Centre at the London Institute (McCallum and Street 1998) and this too has shaped the content of this edition. But the major influence has been the array of recommendations and guidance offered to subject leaders and middle managers by the Teacher Training Authority (TTA), the DfEE and QCA since the first edition, particularly the expectations and requirements held of subject leaders outlined in the Standards for Subject Leaders published by the TTA in 1998. In the light of the Standards document amendments have been made and new sections on skills and competences have been added to Chapters 3 to 8.

The 1998 Report by Her Majesty's Chief Inspector points out that the culture of schools continues to change. More primary schools are moving away from reliance on the single class teacher in order to utilise the particular subject knowledge and enthusiasms of individual teachers. The White Paper (Cm 3681) of 1997 has laid out the national targets to be reached by 2002. Much is expected of middle managers in the intervening years.

Subject leaders will be involved with their headteachers in the identification of school targets and these will inform the individual Development Plans required of all LEAs. The decision has been made to 'focus the curriculum at key stages 1 and 2 on the five subjects of English, Maths, Science, I.T. and R.E. in order to allow primary schools to have more time to deliver the challenging but essential literacy and numeracy targets set for 2002' (DfEE Circular 13 January 1998). The statutory requirement for schools to follow the key stage 1 and 2 programmes of study for design and technology, history, geography, music, art and physical education has been lifted until a revised National Curriculum is brought in from September 2000. Middle managers responsible for subjects outside the core will receive guidance from the QCA in due course. The quality of teaching and learning in non-core subjects will continue to be monitored during OFSTED inspections.

# Introduction

## THE KEY PURPOSE OF THE BOOK

This book seeks to assist teachers in primary and middle schools who are charged, as part of their conditions of service, to take on school-wide responsibilities in addition to their role as classteachers. Some, but not all, of such teachers receive additional salary points on the standard national scale (SNS) in acknowledgement of the work they undertake in such roles as curriculum coordinator, key stage coordinator or curriculum consultant. A good deal of additional work was placed on their shoulders in the wake of the Education Reform Act and the introduction of the National Curriculum. They were the first to cope with the blizzard of paper which ensued and worked hard on behalf of their colleagues to implement the changes.

The Audit Commission Report of 1989 drew attention to ways in which the quality of provision in schools might be assessed and monitored. Since that time OFSTED publications have continued to refer to the role to be played by middle managers in the management and monitoring of the school and its work, and in 1994 coined the term 'subject-manager'. The 1994 School Teachers' Review Body drew attention to the issue in this way:

> OFSTED told us that in primary schools the quality of development plans had improved, with many of the primary schools it had inspected having satisfactory plans produced after appropriate consultation and discussion. Although management structures were generally satisfactory, OFSTED noted that the management tasks most frequently neglected in primary schools were those of monitoring and evaluating the standards achieved and the quality of work in the classroom. There was a need for a stronger evaluative dimension if the schools were to assess whether or not they had reached their goals. High standards were associated with good subject co-ordination and effective leadership from the headteacher. (paragraph 121)

These expectations are not easily achieved. The argument running through this book is that it is extremely difficult for middle managers to undertake such roles in the individualized manner urged by successive reports since 1967. What is needed is a whole-school framework which informs action together with the adoption of a mixed economy of task and role structures which are in keeping with the culture of primary schools. Such a framework is presented in Chapter 3 in which the role to be undertaken by middle managers in the implementation of policy and monitoring of quality is explored in depth. Subsequent chapters seek to assist the development of skills required in the job. The key purpose is to present a viable framework for action by teachers whose non-teaching time is strictly limited. It is hoped that the rationale presented will find favour with headship teams and middle managers in primary schools and assist them in their endeavours during a time in which they have been continually exposed to the constant drip of negative comment from central government and the media.

## ORIGINS

This book is one outcome of an extensive series of development programmes for coordinators in primary schools mounted by QMS (Quality Management for Schools) in three London Boroughs during 1993 and 1994. Most of these programmes were linked to concurrent programmes for primary headteachers and assistant headteachers which varied in length from two to ten days. The programmes were committed to the view that the purpose of management in schools is to improve the quality of the learning experiences offered to pupils. Our shared concern was with the development of relevant strategies, insights and competences needed to meet the challenge of managing schools in the 1990s.

Colleagues were willing to share their practice, to submit it to the critical scrutiny of their peers and in the light of this, to explore constructive and challenging alternatives. Many issues were raised but four were consistently identified:

- the part played by a school's culture in shaping the behaviour of individuals;
- the centrality of an agreed policy for teaching and learning;
- policy formulation and implementation;
- what might constitute an optimum organizational/management structure in schools of different size.

Headteachers also wanted to explore ways in which the quality of the curriculum-in-action might be monitored and assessed. The complexities associated with monitoring and evaluation were acknowledged and in the course of exploring alternatives, four key questions arose:

- How is a whole-school policy for teaching and learning best formulated and what is the role of middle managers during the process of implementation?
- How is a constructive and rigorous monitoring process best introduced? Or, to put it another way, how do we systematize and develop the informal, naturalistic monitoring which already goes on?
- What skills and competences might middle managers need to develop and how might they best be acquired?
- How might the work of middle managers be made more manageable given the constraints of time?

Programmes for coordinators began with a briefing meeting attended by participants and their headteachers, followed by a residential weekend and a further day linked by school-based tasks. Particular attention was paid to the whole-school framework, policy-related observation, analysis and the provision of feedback. Constructive, manageable monitoring linked to developmental initiatives was seen as the main means of achieving policy implementation. Additional single-day workshops were provided for staff in participant schools to support monitoring strategies initiated by the headteachers and assistant headteachers who had attended earlier programmes.

## WHAT IS MEANT BY MIDDLE MANAGEMENT?

The words 'middle management' and 'middle manager' are used throughout the book to refer to members of staff in primary schools who have oversight of a designated area of the curriculum or an aspect of the work of a school such as a key stage, pupil assessment, parent-school liaison, special needs, links with industry, etc. The TTA uses the term subject leader for 'coordinator' and 'scale-post' is normally referred to as a 'responsibility allowance'. Many assistant headteachers also take on a middle manager role in addition to those associated with headship.

The term 'middle manager' is used to reflect a situation in which individual teachers take on a leader-manager role which is then asserted within a group of professional peers. Their job is that of working with and through others in pursuit of particular goals. They are essentially agents who work on behalf of the whole staff in the interests of pupils, parents and other stakeholders in the enterprise we call a school. As they do so they enter into dialogue with the headteacher, or headship team, or senior management team, who are accountable for the effectiveness and efficiency of the overall management and administration of the school. Many middle managers (particularly those having oversight of a curriculum area) occupy reciprocal roles, a fact which makes it all the more important for their combined work to be coordinated at the whole-school level.

Use of the term middle manager should not be seen as implying that some form of hierarchical management is being proposed. Indeed, one of the purposes of the first two chapters is to challenge the viability of a model which frequently overloads individual members of staff with expectations which become difficult, if not impossible, to fulfil.

## THE STRUCTURE OF THE BOOK

The book is presented in three parts, each made up of three chapters. It concludes with an Appendix containing a range of school documents relating to monitoring and observation, together with a draft policy for teaching and learning.

### Part I. Origins, expectations and a framework for development

Part I is made up of three chapters containing five activities relevant to the middle manager role in school. Chapters 1 and 2 explore the emergence of the scale-post system within primary schools and outline the expectations held of middle managers in a series of contemporary reports. The powerful, shaping effect of a school's culture on the actions of its members is then explored and the assumptions underpinning a system of differentiated posts are questioned. Alternative forms of organizational structure are then explored and a mixed economy of project teams and individual roles is proposed as a means of reducing overload. Chapter 3 is probably the most important chapter in the book since it outlines in detail an overarching framework for development, policy implementation and the monitoring of quality in the curriculum-in-action. Key tasks are identified and the role of middle managers in these processes is clearly outlined.

### Part II. Making it happen

Part II is made up of three chapters which focus on the process skills needed by middle managers as they engage in implementing policy, monitoring and the provision of feedback. Approaches to monitoring and development in schools of different size are outlined as well as a range of different ways in which the monitoring process might be started. Six activities are provided for middle managers wishing to explore some of the process skills which have been outlined.

## Part III. Developing skills

The argument for a different approach to middle management in primary schools having been developed in Parts I and II, Part III focuses on additional skills required in the job. The emphasis here is on preparing for the role of leading the team, delegation, the management of change, carrying out school-based evaluation, finance/resource management, self management and the management of time. Part III concludes with an exploration of coordinator-governor relationships and forms of school-parent partnership. Part III also contains 14 activities for exploration and application by the interested middle manager.

# ACKNOWLEDGEMENTS

Thanks are due to all the participants in the various programmes who were willing to share their experiences of middle management. It is not possible to name them all but the contributions of the following colleagues are gratefully acknowledged:

Particular thanks are due to Mike Jolley who, despite extensive commitments, made many valued comments on successive drafts.

London Borough of Croydon: Mike Jolley, David Garrard, Angela Wheatley, David Winters, Karen Leng, Tony Pratchett and Linda Rowan.

London Borough of Enfield: John Jenkins, Ray Arnold, Eve Boyd, Jan Minchella, Peter Stretton and Bridie Weston.

East Sussex LEA: Keith Remnant, Hellen Ward, Judy Grahame and Isobel McNaught-Davis.

Hampshire LEA: John Clouting, Judy Cooper and Kevin Harcombe.

Berkshire LEA: Helen McMullen.

Metropolitan Borough of Stockport: David Baker, Ed Blundell, Alex Hoskins, John Draper and Paul Jackson.

Barking and Dagenham LEA: Mike Hindle and Ken Parry.

Waltham Forest LEA: Scilla Furey, Shirley French and Tim Coulson.

London Borough of Barnet: Pat Marvel.

London Borough of Merton: Stephen Smith, Jenny Smith, Peter Holdsworth and Alan Malarkey.

University of Sussex: David Burrell and Terry Sexton.

Thanks are also due to Hayley Kirby who prepared all the diagrams and figures.

Grateful acknowledgement is made to the following who kindly granted permission for the use of extracts:

Barbara Martin, Sales and Rights Manager, Open University Press for extracts from *What's Worth Fighting For in Your School?* by M. Fullan and A. Hargreaves (1992), cited in Chapter 2.

Ms H. Sternberg, Senior Publications Officer, OFSTED for extracts from *Curriculum Organization and Classroom Practice in Primary Schools* (1992), the follow up report to the latter (1993) and *Primary Matters* (1994).

Mr R. Davies, Publishing Manager, School Curriculum and Assessment Authority for permission to quote from *Planning the Curriculum at Key Stages 1 and 2* (1995).

*Part I*

# Origins, Expectations and a Framework for Development

*Chapter 1*

# In the beginning: the origins and expectations of middle managers in primary schools

This chapter seeks to provide a backcloth to a deeper analysis of the role of coordinators or 'subject/key stage managers' and is presented in three sub-sections:

Beginnings – which covers the period 1900-1944;
The establishment of graded post in primary schools – in the period 1956 to the mid-1970s; and
Middle management in the 1990s – in which contemporary issues are identified and explored and a model of the coordinator role presented.

It will be argued that the introduction of scale-posts in primary schools was a consequence of expediency rather than the outcome of a full consideration of their appropriateness in the primary sector. Contemporary expectations held of middle managers are then explored. The chapter concludes with activities for use in school-based INSET sessions or for use in private study by middle managers.

'Middle management' is used as a convenient term to cover a variety of situations in which designated members of staff accept responsibility for the achievement of corporate goals by working with and through others. Such goals have to be pursued in schools which are markedly different in terms of their size and cultural characteristics and most middle managers have a full-time teaching commitment within a particular year group. 'Middle manager' seems to suggest that primary schools are characterized by hierarchical forms of organization, whereas the reality in most is that of individual teachers with designated responsibilities working in responsive fashion. It is used here to reflect conceptions of roles and responsibilities which have been commonly assumed or implied in reports and literature originating from the DfEE, HMI, OFSTED, QCA, and TTA.

## BEGINNINGS

The origins of differentiated posts in primary schools are to be found in the long and complex history of salary negotiations in which differentiated posts were created first in the grammar schools and then in comprehensive and secondary modern schools in the period between 1906 and 1956. The two processes of role differentiation and professional stratification were witnessed, first in the secondary sector and then, after 1956, in the primary sector. Role differentiation refers to the process whereby the basic role of the teacher is extended as new roles emerge within the school system. Examples in secondary schools would be roles such as Head of House, Head of

Department, Faculty Head and more recent instances such as Assessment Coordinator, Site Manager, Finance Manager, Appraisal Manager, Key Stage coordinator, or Special Needs Coordinator. Professional stratification on the other hand refers to the tendency towards an increased number of status and/or salary levels within schools.

Between 1900 and 1919 salary negotiations were conducted at local level through the actions of local associations of teachers supported by their national executive committees. The 1902 Education Act enabled Counties and County Boroughs to establish secondary schools. Two years later the Assistant Masters Association (AMA) proposed a salary scheme and sought its adoption by local authorities and the governing bodies of endowed schools. Paragraph 2(b) of their proposal provides evidence of an early claim for status differentiation:

> 2(b) Salaries on a higher scale should be paid to members who are specially qualified by attainment or experience and to holders of the following posts (1) second master (2) heads of department (3) head of lower school.

> 2(c) So far as can be done without injury to the interests of the school, these better paid posts should be given to members of staff of long standing and meritorious service.

In 1906 the London County Council adopted a scale of salaries in response to the proposals of the AMA but the practice was by no means universal. The Burnham Committee, so called after its first Chairman, Lord Burnham, was constituted in 1919 and had separate committees for elementary and secondary schools. In the course of the next 50 years the teacher unions successively argued for differentiated posts which reflected the academic and/or pastoral work undertaken by secondary teachers. Their role in preparing pupils for examinations, in managing academic departments and contributing to the management of the school were frequently cited. The National Association of Schoolmasters (NAS), The Association of Assistant Masters and Mistresses (AMMA) and the National Union of Teachers (NUT) pressed the case for parity of esteem between different types of secondary school and the provision of equivalent roles in secondary modern, grammar and comprehensive schools. By the mid-1960s there were comparable roles available to teachers within each of the different kinds of secondary school.

The agenda of the elementary committee of Burnham moved to a different beat. The establishment of the Burnham structure was in fact a direct response to teacher strikes which occurred in more than 30 areas during 1918 and 1919. The effects of the militant action taken by elementary teachers is reflected in the comments of the President of the Board of Education, Lord Fisher, in the Commons:

> In spite of the fact that the system of elementary school finance is now based on a principle definitely framed to encourage education authorities to be liberal in their salaries, in spite of the very liberal superannuation which has now been granted to teachers … there is still considerable unrest and this unrest has been giving me very serious concern. There have been strikes here and strikes there and the work of the local education authorities whose attention ought now to be engaged in the very difficult problems created by the Education Act (of 1917) is greatly embarrassed by these salary disputes. I have endeavoured to find some means by which these disputes might be minimised and the atmosphere generally sweetened. (*Hansard*, 12 August 1919, cols 1231–2)

The major item on the elementary teachers' agenda at this time was the need for a national scale of remuneration and the elimination of a system with different grades of teacher (trained certificated; untrained certificated; uncertificated; supplementary).

The separate elementary and secondary Committees of Burnham were abolished in 1944 when a new Burnham Committee comprised of a Teachers Panel and an Authorities Panel was created in their place. The 1944 Act had secured a national scale for all teachers and one consequence of this was further diversification in the arguments presented by the different professional associations as each projected the interests of its members in the new forum.

## THE ESTABLISHMENT OF GRADED POSTS IN PRIMARY SCHOOLS

Differentiated posts first became available in a small number of large primary schools in 1956, some 50 years after their emergence in the secondary sector. It is not too fanciful to suggest that graded posts in primary schools were a by-product of salary negotiations. An impasse in the Burnham negotiations of 1956 prompted Lord Alexander to propose that the current system of graded salary scales be replaced by graded posts of responsibility linked to a school's 'Unit Total System' (UTS). Under UTS each pupil was worth a number of points according to age. The total score for a school determined the school's group for salary purposes. Pupils under 13 counted as one point and pupils between 13 and 15, two points. Three levels of graded post were introduced, each with its associated allowance, according to a school's score under the UTS. The age weighting favoured schools with older pupils, and large schools with the oldest pupils were the main beneficiaries of the 1956 Burnham Agreement. The format effectively doubled the unit totals of secondary modern schools, a fact which helped promote the case for parity of esteem between different kinds of secondary school. Head of Department posts could only be established in secondary schools. Such posts were mandatory in schools having GCE 'O' level courses, and permissible in schools where there were no such courses (so much for parity of esteem!) For more than three quarters of primary schools the 1956 settlement made no difference. Under its terms only 12.2 per cent of primary schools qualified for a deputy headteacher plus one graded post, 6.5 per cent for a deputy and two posts, 2.7 per cent for a deputy and three posts, and only 1.3 per cent for more than three posts and a deputy. Nevertheless an important principle had been established and from that date onwards, salary negotiations resulted in the progressive expansion of such posts in the primary sector. Figure 1.1 shows the rate of increase in the period 1968 to 1977.

From 1963 onwards the process of stratification, already established in comprehensive and secondary modern schools, was replicated in all but the smallest of primary schools. It became possible to appoint Heads of Department in primary schools in 1963 and these were often used to acknowledge the work undertaken by teachers who had oversight of an infant department in a JMI school. In successive awards the number of scale posts was increased. In 1971 all references to 'undertaking special responsibility' were dropped from Burnham Reports. From that time there was an increasing mismatch between observations made on the role of post holders in such publications as the Plowden Report (1967) or the Bullock Report (1975), and practices adopted in schools in appointing and determining the

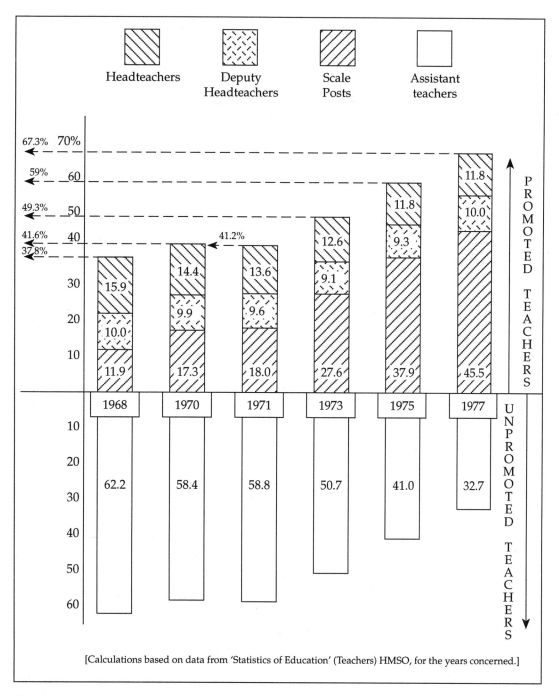

**Figure 1.1**    The growth of professional stratification in primary schools 1968–1977

responsibilities of scale post holders. From the mid-1970s headteachers were obliged to award, in consultation with their LEA, a fixed proportion of scale posts in accordance with the terms of successive Burnham Agreements. In many medium to large primary schools (schools with more than 350 pupils) there were almost as many scale posts as there were members of staff, a situation which led, in some instances, to posts being awarded to retain the services of experienced staff particularly during periods of teacher shortage. The situation is reflected in the experience of one teacher at that time in these words:

As a teacher in the mid-seventies I was one of a number of staff who were on salary scales 2 or 3. Many of my colleagues regarded their promotion as an acknowledgement of long service and loyalty to the school. We regarded our posts as a mark of status. Some were year leaders and some had responsibility for a subject but for most of us the duties were nominal rather than real. (Author's fieldnotes, 1979)

Promotion to Scale 2 posts in the mid-1970s was not always a rigorous process, as indicated in these extracts from interviews carried out by the author at the time:

NW    Were you interviewed for the post?

Mrs G    Good heavens no. I was given it. I didn't apply for it. I wouldn't have been having one if that was the case. I was the longest serving member of staff and it was a sort of recognition for what I had done for the school. That's how the Head put it to me. I was quite surprised to find that it was for needlework and country dancing that they actually tied it down to, which was what I did at the time....

NW    How did you get the job?

Mr W    I was just told by the headteacher. He just came up and said, 'You've got it, there's a teacher going on secondment'. I was on dinner duty at the time and I didn't know what he was talking about at first. (Fieldwork data, N.West, University of Sussex, 1979)

In 1978 the Department of Education and Science (DES) published *Primary Education in England* based on a survey carried out by HMI. The survey presented an account of some aspects of the work of 7-, 9-, and 11-year-old children in 542 schools so chosen as to be representative of primary schools in England. The survey was published in the wake of Labour Prime Minister James Callaghan's Ruskin speech which set in train the 'Great Debate' on standards in education and raised calls for greater accountability within schools and between schools and parents. As part of their survey, HMI commented on the work and influence exerted by teachers with special curricular responsibilities and noted that in only one quarter of the schools in the survey:

were teachers with positions of curricular or organizational responsibility having a noticeable influence on the quality of work in the school as a whole. In the remaining schools there was little evidence that the influence of such teachers spread beyond the work in their own classrooms. (para 4.5)

From that point onwards successive surveys (DES, 1979; 1982; 1983; 1985; 1989; 1993; 1994) have assiduously asserted that in all schools heads and deputies have a major leadership role to play, as have staff undertaking the role of curriculum advisers in primary, first and middle schools.

The Burnham Committee, which had presided over teachers' pay since 1919, was replaced by an Interim Advisory Committee on Pay and Conditions following the enactment of the 1988 Education Reform Act. This interim committee was superseded by the School Teachers' Review Body which reports annually on matters relating to teachers' pay. Following the phased introduction of the Local Management of Schools (LMS) after 1988, school governing bodies have responsibility for the financial management of schools. In maintained schools the LEA is the employer of the staff but the governing body and the head have separate and particular responsibilities for selection and staff management. Where a school has a delegated budget, the LEA cannot lay down a staffing complement for it. When a member of staff leaves, it is the governors who have the final decision on whether a replacement is to be made. The LEA may give advice and governing bodies must take this into account when considering appointments. The current situation, as stated in the Teachers' Pay & Conditions Document 1997 is as follows:

> The relevant body may award up to 5 full points to a classroom teacher who undertakes specific responsibilities beyond those common to the majority of teachers. (para 10.3)

In addition,

> The relevant body may award up to 3 full points for excellent performance, having regard to all aspects of the classroom teacher's professional duties but in particular to classroom teaching. (para 10.4)

The TTA framework for Continuing Professional Development includes a category 'Extended Skills Teacher'. Implementation problems have yet to be resolved and limitations on the size of school budgets make it difficult to pay such awards. 'Extended Skill' teachers need careful deployment since taking them out of their classroom too frequently defeats the objective.

Throughout the long history of salary negotiations there has been a reluctance within the profession to link additional allowances to excellence as a classroom practitioner, a practice regarded by the professional associations as divisive and unhelpful. The recommendation is still resisted today. The 1994 School Teacher's Review Body Report noted:

> schools continue to have strong reservations about the principle and practicality of rewarding excellence; and a number of LEAs have discouraged schools from awarding excellence points. (para 59)

## MIDDLE MANAGEMENT IN THE 1990s

The context in which post holders now undertake their work is very different from the situation at the time of the national survey carried out between 1975 and 1977 and published as *Primary Education in England: A Survey by H.M. Inspectors of Schools* (DES, 1978). Schools are required to implement the National Curriculum and in doing so receive advice from the Office for Standards in Education (OFSTED) and the School Curriculum and Assessment Authority (QCA). The powers of the Secretary of State for Education have been substantially increased in successive legislation since the passing of the 1988 Education Reform Act.

In 1992, a Discussion Paper entitled *Curriculum Organization and Classroom Practice*, was produced by Alexander, Rose and Woodhead at the behest of the Secretary of State. This was followed by two further discussion documents published by OFSTED, *Curriculum Organization and Classroom Practice, A Follow-up Report* (1993), and *Primary Matters, A Discussion on Teaching and Learning in Primary Schools* (1994), both of which drew on information gathered by HMI in samples of schools. These three documents, together with *The Handbook for the Inspection of Schools* (OFSTED, 1993, revised 1994 and 1995), provide important contemporary reference points concerning the management of the curriculum in primary schools. They also outline the curriculum leadership role to be undertaken by headteachers and their deputies. More importantly for the concerns of this book, they outline a set of expectations in relation to members of staff who have been given responsibility for the management of particular subjects or who undertake a specific functional role. The key points from the first three documents are outlined below.

## Curriculum Organization and Classroom Practice in Primary Schools, Alexander, Rose and Woodhead (1992)

This report reviewed available evidence about the delivery of education in primary schools in order to make recommendations about curriculum organization, teaching methods and classroom practice appropriate for the successful implementation of the National Curriculum, particularly at Stage 2. In the view of the authors, 'The time is now right to examine the appropriateness of existing models of curriculum organization, teaching methodology and staff deployment in the light of the National Curriculum requirements' (para 57). With reference to curriculum leaders/coordinators: 'The idea of the curriculum co-ordinator was developed to try to ensure that a school could make maximum use of the collective subject strength of its staff ... In principle the curriculum co-ordinator ought, in the larger school at least, to be able to sustain the work of the generalist teacher' (paras 78/79).

The authors acknowledged that coordinators had had a significant impact on whole school planning and resource management, but were conscious that the limited non-contact time and the level of skill and sensitivity required in the role meant that they had had less influence on actual classroom practice. The educational leadership of the headteacher was regarded as crucial and, given the range of subjects to be covered, it was suggested that,

> headteachers should delegate responsibilities for subject co-ordination and development to other members of staff...They need to spell out the responsibilities and accountabilities of co-ordinators thoroughly and provide support to enable them to discharge their executive responsibilities. Co-ordinators should be given opportunities to lead working groups, produce curriculum guidance, order resources, provide INSET, inform the planning and work of colleagues by working alongside them in class and take part in the monitoring and evaluation of their subjects across the school...Regular monitoring and evaluation of classroom practice by headteachers play a major part in assessing the effectiveness of co-ordinators and contributed to the regular appraisal of their work (para 159).

## OFSTED follow-up report to Alexander, Rose and Woodhead (1993)

This report summarizes 'the extensive discussion of the issues about classroom organisation and classroom practice that has taken place since the publication of the paper and comments upon the extent of any changes made and their impact in the primary schools and classes observed by HMI over that period'. In relation to coordinators the report states: 'Most of the schools had curriculum coordinators with clearly defined roles. In a significant number of schools, their influence on teachers' planning was evident. However, due to a lack, or poor use, of non-contact time they were able to take little part in the monitoring of work in classrooms.' The two issues, of monitoring and non-contact time, are of crucial importance and it is not surprising that they were focused upon in the third report, *Primary Matters*.

**Primary Matters – A Discussion on Teaching and Learning in Primary Schools (OFSTED, 1994)**

This publication reports the findings of a survey 'focusing on primary matters related to the quality of teaching and from that basis raises a number of important general issues mainly concerned with curriculum and staff management and development'. The survey was conducted in 49 schools variously located and ranging in size from 6 to 540 pupils on roll. The schools 'appeared to be broadly representative of primary schools nationally'. Examples of coordinator practice cited in the report included:
- involvement in the long- or medium-term planning of topics and subjects;
- acting as a semi-specialist teacher, teaching every class in the school their own subject for a block of three weeks out of every 12;
- giving demonstration lessons;
- working alongside colleagues;
- preparing and introducing a series of lessons for a whole year group;
- writing policies and schemes of work;
- leading staff meetings;
- providing INSET;
- attending courses;
- auditing, purchasing and organizing resources;
- advising teachers;
- supporting or leading planning.

*Primary Matters*, para. 35, outlines the work to be undertaken by the headteacher in managing the curriculum. This is reproduced here in full since it provides the backcloth to the work of coordinators:

The work of the headteacher in managing the curriculum involves:
i  Co-ordination.
- developing an agreed view of what constitutes the school curriculum and its relationship to the National Curriculum;
- identifying principles and procedures for interrelating the constituent parts of the curriculum;
- setting out principles and procedures for making and implementing curriculum decisions;
- establishing the roles and responsibilities of all those involved in curriculum decision making;
- organizing the curriculum to help
  - achieve the aims of the school;
  - provide coverage of the statutory curriculum;
  - promote the educational achievement of pupils.
ii. Monitoring.
- monitoring teachers' planning and preparation to ensure appropriate coverage of the attainment targets and programmes of study of the statutory curriculum and to ensure coverage of the other aspects of the school's agreed curriculum;
- monitoring the work undertaken in classes to see how the work planned and prepared is actually transacted and assessed.
iii Evaluation.
Using the OFSTED Framework for Inspection and other sources,
- evaluating the whole curriculum using the criteria of breadth, balance, continuity,

progression, coherence and compliance with National Curriculum requirements;

- evaluating the teaching techniques and organizational strategies employed, using the criterion of fitness of purpose;
- evaluating the standards and progress achieved by individuals and groups and looking for trends and patterns of achievement;
- evaluating the overall quality of the education provided, including extra-curricular activities;
- evaluating the standards achieved and the quality of the education provided.

In noting the key tasks of headteachers outlined in *Primary Matters* it is important to acknowledge that in the period 1988 to 1993 they have had to bring LMS on stream, manage the implementation of the National Curriculum and introduce staff appraisal. The introduction of LMS and appraisal were phased initiatives whose precise timing was largely determined by LEAs. LMS constituted a sea change for most schools. The diversity of changes and the rapidity with which they were introduced understandably resulted in a good deal of reactive management and it is hardly surprising that some headteachers were distracted from the core task of curriculum leadership.

### The role of the subject-manager

The report suggests that 'in all but the smallest primary schools headteachers are able to delegate the management of particular subjects to individual members of staff'. A major shift is then suggested:

> In terms of the management responsibilities, teachers who are subject managers for the whole school ('Coordinators' is too limited a description) can be expected to (a) develop a clear view of the nature of their subject and its contribution to the wider curriculum of the school; (b) to provide advice and documentation to help teachers to teach the subject and interrelate its constituent elements; and (c) to play a major part in organising the teaching and the resources of the subject so that statutory requirements are covered. These aspects of the subject manager's role can largely be discharged outside the teaching day but while they require little or no non-contact time they do need a considerable investment of time and energy. (para. 37)

The report accepts the need for non-contact time to be made available if subject managers are to undertake monitoring:

> The monitoring of teaching, learning and assessment practices requires non-contact time for subject managers. Subject managers can also be expected to contribute to the overall evaluation of work in their subject against agreed criteria, to evaluate standards of achievements and to identify trends and patterns in pupils' performance. Such contributions to evaluation are more valid if informed by the firsthand experience of monitoring work in classes but can also be based, at least in part, on the examination of the teachers' and children's work. (para. 38)

Auditing curriculum time and the deployment of staff are also identified as important issues. Monitoring the time allocated to different subjects in different classes is seen as a task best undertaken by headteachers, aided by subject managers.

## Issues relating to a subject-manager approach

If we take an historical perspective on middle management roles in primary schools it is possible to regard them as the outcome of an expedient political decision and, once established, they were consistently and persistently argued for on grounds of parity of opportunity between the primary and secondary sectors. Primary schools were expected to mirror secondary schools in terms of differentiated roles. The cultural features of primary schools seem to have been largely disregarded. The inimical features reported by HMI in 1978 *could* have been analysed in terms of the *inappropriateness* of a designated role model in primary schools. HMI *could* have recommended the adoption of a *task or team culture* which may have been a far more productive way forward. Reports at this time present a stance of 'more of the same (i.e. designated roles) only better', in relation to curriculum management, monitoring and evaluation, rather than encouraging schools to explore *different* ways of achieving such goals. A 'mixed economy' may still prove to be the best way forward.

Implementing the recommendations of *Primary Matters* will be not be easy. Unlike secondary schools, where the operational unit is a department, primary subject managers in medium to large schools may often be relating to much larger groups of staff than their secondary counterparts, without the advantage of a common subject identity. Under the terms of teachers' conditions of service all members of staff are expected to undertake responsibility over and above that of being a classteacher, irrespective of whether they receive additional recompense. In addition, in all but the smallest of schools, there will be members of staff with designated roles relating to the different curriculum areas. The supply of teachers is such that it is unlikely that any one school will have been able to designate such roles to staff who possess the relevant formal qualifications in the subjects concerned. Many teachers have recognized the gaps in subject expertise that exist within their schools and have been willing to take up the shortfall on the basis of an interest in the subject. Many such teachers will have taken advantage of 'top up' courses designed to assist them in their endeavours. There is little doubt of the impressive role played by such teachers in the period following the Education Reform Act of 1988, when they were the first to grapple with the complexities of the National Curriculum and engage in the transposition of programmes of study, and statutory and non-statutory guidance as the basis for implementing the new orders.

Adoption of the designated role model outlined by OFSTED is not a simple matter, even if the resources to support the appropriate non-contact time were to be made available within the constraints of a school's budget share. It is impossible for individual coordinators to fulfil the expectations held of them unless they are empowered by a headteacher who has established the appropriate conditions. The age of the heroic leader-manager is dead. Headteachers can only fulfil the wide range of tasks outlined in *Primary Matters* by delegating authority to act in ways which are understood and valued by all members of the team. If we are to take seriously the need to engage in monitoring, review and evaluation it is necessary for all members of staff to understand such processes and acquire competence in such aspects as data collection, observation, analysis and feedback plus the capacity to structure and present evaluation reports which assist decision making. The role as defined by OFSTED is complex; to illustrate this a model of the key functions of subject coordinator/managers is presented in Figure 1.2 which is presented in the form of a revolving wheel in order to reflect the dynamics of the coordinator's work setting. Six sectors make up the 'spokes' of the wheel, each 'spoke' linking explicit policies to the ongoing process of regular, systematic monitoring of the policies in action at the faster moving rim. Each of the six sectors is interrelated as indicated by the broken lines. The pupil is located at the centre of the wheel to remind us that pupils and their needs constitute the *raison d'être* for a school. Explicit teaching and learning policies are located at the more slowly turning hub since they, together with schemes of work, inform practice and fuel the monitoring process. Such policies reflect the core function of the school, namely, the promotion of quality learning. The figure presents each of the six areas in equal proportion, but at any one point in time coordinators will be focusing on some sectors rather than others. All sectors need to be effectively managed. Some may be on 'hold' whilst in others the coordinator may be engaged in developmental initiatives of various kinds. The TTA published National Standards for Subject Leaders in 1998 and these were outlined under five headings :

1. Core purpose of subject leadership.
2. Key outcomes of subject leadership.
3. Professional knowledge and understanding.
4. Skills and attitudes.
5. Key areas of subject leadership.

Each of theses aspects are covered in Chapters 3 to 9.

## Subject/pedagogy

This is the area of personal and professional development in which the individual constructs, over time, their vision of a particular subject area and its contribution to the curriculum as a whole. Such a vision is based on subject knowledge and a clearly articulated appreciation of what constitutes high quality teaching and learning in the curriculum area concerned. It is informed by critical reflection on matters of practice, dialogue with significant colleagues within and outside the school, and membership of relevant professional and subject associations.

Analysis of questionnaires completed by curriculum coordinators in three LEAs during development programmes led by the author revealed that a substantial number had been required to change their designated curriculum area more than once, a situation which makes the subject knowledge aspect of their role problematic. One third had two or more curriculum areas to manage, which exacerbates the situation. Managing more than one curriculum area is, however, a fact of life for teachers in small primary schools.

### Advice, documentation and support

In this area coordinators are involved in such processes as: policy formulation, implementation and/or review; formulating or revising schemes of work; assisting the planning process by leading or advising year-group teams as they construct units of work, lesson plans, projects and themes; working alongside colleagues; offering advice; assisting in the induction of new staff; assisting and leading school-based INSET initiatives; preparing guidelines according to need; and making contributions to the school development plan. They will also be expected to provide documentation relevant to an LEA or OFSTED inspection.

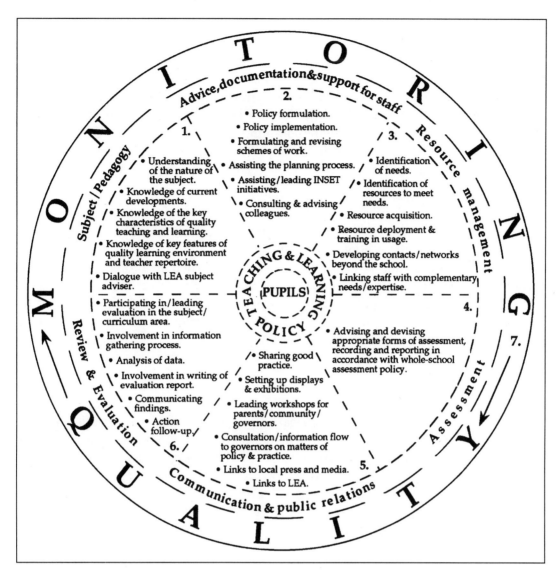

**Figure 1.2**    Key elements of the coordinator/subject manager role

*Resource management*

This area reflects the 'servicing' function undertaken by coordinators who are concerned with the effective use of teaching and learning resources. This will involve them in the process of needs-identification, the subsequent acquisition and deployment of materials and equipment and the maintenance of same. Needs-based resource management calls into play the need for consultation and dialogue with colleagues. The monitoring of resources-in-use provides a useful and relatively unthreatening way of engaging in more systematic approaches to monitoring at whole-school level. Effective resource management embraces much more than provisioning and includes the development of strategies for teaching and learning, the use of the environment and the constructive and imaginative involvement of members of the local community. Developing networks and establishing contacts across the boundary of the school are important aspects of their work.

*Assessment*

Many schools have designated assessment coordinators who work in consultation with the staff to produce whole-school policies for assessment, recording and reporting. Dialogue with subject coordinators has enabled them to devise appropriate forms of recording and reporting across the curriculum. Many coordinators have been involved in the sampling of pupils' work, agreement trialling and the development of pupil portfolios as part of their monitoring function.

*Communication and public relations*

The first level of communication relates to the identification and dissemination of good practice within the school. This is likely to involve the coordinator in setting up displays and exhibitions to meet the needs of particular audiences. It is now common practice for coordinators to present reports to the governing body and to advise them on matters of policy and practice in the course of governor visits to the school. Coordinators frequently provide valuable information to the school's press/media officer on subjects of mutual interest.

*Evaluation*

Systematic evaluation requires a good deal of time and energy and in consequence is best engaged in periodically. Much will depend upon the scale of a particular evaluation but it is unlikely that the process could be successfully undertaken by a single member of staff. A coordinator might lead an evaluation but it will involve most, if not all, the members of the school at some point, either as data-gatherers or respondents. All staff need to understand the process if they are to make an effective contribution.

*Monitoring*

This process is located on the circumference of the wheel since monitoring is regarded as an ongoing and systematic feature of the school. Monitoring answers the question: 'Do we do what we say that we do?' and, in relation to the curriculum-in-action, refers to the means that are used to check that agreed shifts in practice and associated learning outcomes are being planned for and celebrated in the classroom. A good deal of monitoring is already carried out by teachers, coordinators and headteachers, but it is often informal and unsystematized. If we are to establish a more overt system it is essential *that the process is regarded as supportive and developmental in its intentions,* and that staff accept the aim of improving congruence between the 'public map' (the policy for teaching and learning) and the 'classroom reality' (the curriculum-in-action as it is implemented by individual members of staff). Monitoring is not the same as evaluation, though the decision to evaluate a particular aspect of teaching and learning might arise as one outcome of monitoring. Monitoring the curriculum-in-action might be compared to taking a series of snapshots or film clips of classrooms and comparing these to the film script of agreed policy.

This seven-fold functional model provides a reference point in discussing issues associated with middle management in primary schools. Is it possible for teachers to undertake such a wide range of responsibilities when they have responsibility for a class for most of their time? Does it represent heavy overload which few, if any, can discharge? How can we meet the range of expectations given the limits on school budgets? There is also the question of the skills required in the role of middle manager. Implementing a subject-manager approach to managing, monitoring and evaluating the curriculum calls for a wide range of skills and competences in the individuals concerned. Many of these can be acquired in the course of school-based development programmes. But it is not simply a matter of skills acquisition and application. The ways in which roles are undertaken are markedly influenced by the culture of the school. Having a job-description is one thing – carrying out a role is another. This aspect is developed in Chapter 2.

The following activities have been found helpful in promoting initial discussion on the role of the curriculum coordinator/subject manager.

---

### Activity 1

### WHERE ARE YOU?

This activity is best carried out in partnership with a colleague who holds a similar post in your school.

If you have a job description read it through, comparing its content with the seven sectors outlined in Figure 1.2. How far does your job description compare to the expectations presented in *Primary Matters* and outlined in the third section of this chapter? Is there much variation between colleagues in similar roles?

Go through each of the aspects outlined in Figure 1.2, ticking off those aspects in which you have been involved this year. How similar are your responses? If there are differences, what do feel accounts for the variation?

Does your job description reflect the reality of what you can actually accomplish in the time available to you?

---

### Activity 2

### KEY TASKS

Job descriptions are written in a variety of ways. Yours may take the form of defining key purposes, key tasks together with associated accountabilities which you are to undertake within a specific time-scale, or it may be expressed in more general terms leaving you to convert the latter into specific tasks. Whatever the form, analyse your job description in terms of key tasks:

What key tasks have you undertaken so far this year?
Have you discussed these tasks at regular intervals with the headteacher or some other nominated member of staff?
Do you know, right now, the key tasks being undertaken by other members of staff?
Do they know what your key tasks are?

---

## OVERVIEW

The emergence of the scale post system in the primary sector has been briefly outlined. Its origins lie in arguments about relative status and role differentiation within the secondary sector, in debates about equity between different kinds of secondary school, and in campaigns which pursued parity of esteem between the primary and secondary sectors. The culmination of all these different strands resulted in the replication of differentiated roles in primary schools after 1956. Professional associations continued to press for an adequate career structure within the primary sector and argued the case for pay scales to reflect the status due to teachers. Throughout the debate there has been a reluctance to link additional allowances to excellence as a classroom practitioner, a practice regarded by the professional associations as divisive and unhelpful.

The main points of three significant reports (DES, 1992; Alexander *et al.*, 1993; and OFSTED, 1994) have been identified. These are the latest in a long line of reports which have endorsed a differentiated role approach to curriculum development, management, monitoring and evaluation. A seven-fold model of the subject manager role has been presented. Such a role requires the acquisition of a range of skills, but the problem should not be construed as one related to these alone. Even where the skills and competences are to hand, much will depend on the culture of the school.

Three activities have been presented which may assist readers interested in exploring the viability of existing approaches to middle management in their schools.

## Chapter 2

# Middle management and the culture of the school

The particular characteristics of a school's culture shape the lives of staff in significant ways. This culture has been defined in terms of:

> the collective programming of the mind that distinguishes the members of one school from another. Cultural life in schools is constructed reality, and leaders play a key part in building this reality. School culture includes values, symbols, beliefs and shared meanings of parents, students, teachers and others conceived as a group or community. Culture governs what is of worth for this group and how members should think, feel and behave. The stuff of culture includes a school's customs and traditions; historical accounts; stated and unstated understandings; habits, norms and expectations; common meanings and shared assumptions. (Sergiovanni and Corbally, 1984)

In the previous chapter it was suggested that successive reports have pressed upon schools a designated role model with associated job descriptions and an expectation that subject managers will undertake a complex functional role with the range of attributes summarized in Figure 1.2. In this chapter the concepts of school *culture* and organizational *structure* will be explored since both affect the manner in which middle management tasks are carried out. A distinction will be made between different kinds of task: *maintenance* tasks and *developmental* tasks. A 'mixed economy' of task teams and designated roles will be suggested as a constructive way of managing, monitoring and evaluating the curriculum.

Handy (1984) suggests that each school has its own mix of four kinds of organizational culture: the role culture, the task culture, the club culture, and the person culture. The role culture is frequently portrayed in the form of a Greek temple in which the pillars represent the different functions or specialities which are overseen by senior management; this is shown in Figure 2.1. If we transpose this representation to the primary school we must immediately make significant changes, as indicated in Figure 2.2.

Most members of staff occupy the role of class teacher for the bulk of their time. This has the net effect of drastically reducing the columns underneath the pediment, the shortness of the pillars representing the time available for individuals to discharge their additional roles and responsibilities. The impression one is left with is that of overloaded pillars, unless of course certain conditions prevail which make a role culture a viable proposition. Where schools have an effective and rigorous role culture (as distinct from schools which have adopted only the rhetoric of a role culture), certain conditions are likely to prevail:

- There is a reasonably close match between the qualifications and/or additional training undertaken by individual members of staff and the areas of the curriculum for which they are accountable.

- Staff taking on the role of curriculum coordinator/manager have first-hand experience of teaching different age groups in the curriculum area concerned, though not necessarily across the key stages.
- Job descriptions are regularly audited so as to avoid overload.
- Key tasks are identified and allocated each term. All staff are aware of such key tasks and the authority which has been given to the staff concerned.
- Sufficient non-contact time has been made available to individual curriculum coordinators to enable them to engage meaningfully in observation, constructive monitoring and support.
- An agreed scheme of work or policy for each subject area is in place and curriculum documentation is clear and succinct.
- The work of coordinator/subject managers is effectively coordinated and sequenced by the headteacher, the deputy headteacher, or both.
- The school is likely to have at least two forms of entry as a JMI school or three forms of entry as a junior school. This seems to generate the 'critical mass' that makes a role culture viable.

(These conditions were identified by headteachers and deputies on QMS development programmes in 1994.)

Whilst role cultures are defined in terms of differentiated functions this does not necessarily imply that the institutions are hierarchical in nature, although they are often portrayed as such in the literature.

It is helpful to distinguish between the *culture* of a school and its organizational *structure*. The latter tells us who is supposed to relate to whom in order to get the work done. The culture of the school will significantly shape those relationships and in primary schools these are likely to be characterized by mutuality and reciprocity rather than a pecking order and relative status. Management structures based on designated roles in an incompatible school culture provide a rhetoric which does not match reality. In such a situation middle managers may find it impossible to undertake the interventionist strategies expected of them. Kinder and Harland (1991) have drawn attention to the demotivating effects which can follow in a situation in which '"ideal" co-ordinator practice is represented as a more interventive consultancy role while "real" coordinators find they can only operate in a very much more humble way' (p.210).

Some form of *task culture* may prove to be a more productive alternative to a role culture, given the reluctance of many coordinators to adopt an interventionist stance towards their colleagues on matters of practice. The organizational idea behind a task culture is that a group or team of talents and resources are applied to a project, problem or task, in such a way that each task gets the treatment it requires. Groups can be changed or disbanded as new problems are identified and dealt with. Many primary schools have tackled the challenges associated with the introduction of the National Curriculum in just such a way, thus illustrating the appropriateness of a task culture. The resolution of problems by such groups has implications for the working practices of the rest of the staff and requires strong forms of collaboration beyond the task groups themselves. In Handy's (1984) research, primary schools scored as almost pure task cultures in their responses to questionnaires whilst observational data suggested that they had many of the characteristics of a benevolent club culture.

Fullan and Hargreaves (1992) have drawn attention to the importance of collaboration and point out that the changes involved in moving towards deep and

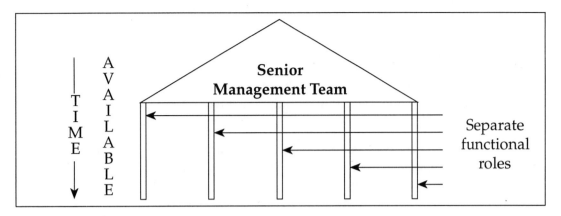

**Figure 2.1**    Idealized role culture (based on C. Handy, 1976)

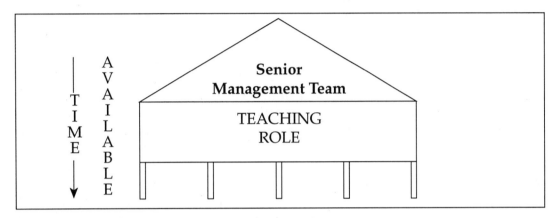

**Figure 2.2**    The reality

effective collaboration are complex, adding that 'the mere existence of collaboration should not be mistaken for a thoroughgoing culture of it'. They noted three forms of collaborative culture:

*Comfortable collaboration* describes a school culture in which forms of collaboration are bounded rather than extended:

Bounded collaboration rarely reaches down to the grounds, the principles or the ethics of practice. It can get stuck with the more comfortable business of advice giving, trick-trading and material-sharing of a more immediate, specific and technical nature. Such collaboration does not extend beyond particular units of work or subjects of study to the wider purpose and value of what is taught and how. It is collaboration which focuses on the immediate, the short term and the practical to the exclusion of longer-term planning concerns. It is collaboration which does not embrace the principles of systematic reflective practice. (p.75)

*Contrived collegiality* is characterized by:

a set of formal, specific bureaucratic procedures to increase the attention being given to joint teacher planning, consultation and other forms of working together. It can be seen in initiatives such as curriculum co-ordinators, mentor schemes, joint-planning in specially provided rooms, school based management and clear job descriptions and training programmes for those in consultative roles...They are meant to encourage greater association among teachers and to foster more sharing, learning and improvement of skills and expertise. Contrived collegiality is also meant to assist the successful implementation of new approaches from the outside into a more responsive and supportive school culture. (p.78)

This form of collaboration may be a first phase in establishing a fully collaborative school culture which is the most extended form, characterized by the fact that:

> failure and uncertainty are not protected and defended, but shared and discussed with a view to gaining help and support. Teachers do not waste time and energy covering their backs here. Collaborative cultures require broad agreement on educational values, but they also tolerate disagreement and to some extent actively encourage it within these limits. Schools characterised by collaborative cultures are also places of hard work, of strong and common commitment, dedication, of collective responsibility, and of a special sense of pride in the institution. (p.66)

Middle managers may be able to play a significant role in changing the organizational culture of their schools but much will depend on the headteacher. The part played by headteachers in shaping a school's culture is frequently cited in the literature on school development and improvement (see for example Holly and Southworth, 1989; West, 1992b; Fullan and Hargreaves, 1992; Hopkins *et al.*, 1994). Middle managers and headteachers seeking to move their school towards more extended forms of collaboration need each other and where this is so, middle managers have increased opportunity to change existing norms. Schein (1985) suggests that culture is created by the actions of leaders, is embedded by leaders and strengthened by them. The pressures experienced by schools in the wake of the 1988 Education Reform Act have resulted in a greater recognition of the value of collaboration and have also increased opportunities for leadership throughout the staff. Schein has indicated how leaders 'may not have the answers, but they must provide temporary stability and emotional reassurance while the answer is being worked out'. A good deal of post-ERA 'working out' has occurred in schools under just such conditions. Most primary heads would agree that this anxiety-containing function has been especially important during the introduction of the National Curriculum, when old habits had to be given up before new ones were learned. In this sense primary headteachers and coordinators need to be skilled managers of change who recognize which cultural features are well adapted to new requirements and which need to be changed.

The strength of well-developed collaborative cultures is that they enable leaders to disclose when their vision is no longer clear and permit them to reformulate the vision through dialogue without loss of face. The process of changing organizational cultures has sometimes been described in terms of 'unfreezing' and 'refreezing'. 'Unfreezing' requires the 'disconfirmation' of current expectations and behaviour, redefining and changing these, and then 'refreezing' the new assumptions. In some schools this will mean that the issue of classroom autonomy and individualism will have to be addressed. For some staff the cult of classroom autonomy is the consequence of years without the benefits of constructive feedback, whilst for others it may be the result of impossibly high self-expectations which have drained them of any energy which might have been available for collective endeavours.

The following activity invites you to consider the culture of your school. You may wish to complete it on your own, but it is a useful exercise to undertake with other members of staff. Some schools have found it useful to ask all members of staff to participate and have used it as the basis for discussions relating to the school's vision statement or to open up the whole question of what kind of culture is being worked towards within the school.

---

### Activity 4

**WHAT ARE THE CULTURAL CHARACTERISTICS OF YOUR SCHOOL?**

Fullan and Hargreaves (1992) have defined school culture as 'the way we do things and relate to one another around here'. Consider your school from such a perspective as you answer the following questions:
- Does your school have some or most of the features of a role culture? Make a list of such features.
- Does your school have any of the characteristics of a task culture? List those characteristics which fit a task culture.
- Consider your school in terms of the three levels of collaboration defined by Fullan and Hargreaves.
- Which description of collaboration best fits your school as it is now?
- What changes in the culture of your school would you wish to support and promote?

---

## MAINTENANCE AND DEVELOPMENT TASKS

Curriculum/subject managers, in addition to their role as class teachers, have seven functions to attend to; these were outlined in Figure 1.2 in the previous chapter:
- subject/pedagogy
- advice, documentation and support for staff
- resource management
- assessment
- communication and public relations
- review and evaluation
- monitoring.

Such functions are achieved through various kinds of task. The overall tasks to be achieved within a school may be divided into two broad categories: maintenance tasks and developmental tasks.

*Maintenance tasks* are those which must be undertaken if the school is to be effective and maintain the quality of *existing* provision. Most of the available energy in organizations is spent on maintenance. The core maintenance task of every member of staff is that of maintaining the quality of teaching and learning. Other maintenance tasks are less complex but are nevertheless essential to the smooth running of the school, such as maintaining record systems, acquiring and servicing teaching and learning resources, planning current work, drawing up rotas, deploying non-teaching and ancillary staff, consulting with parents, coordinating meetings, providing reports to various audiences, or organizing annual events.

*Developmental tasks* are tasks concerned with taking the school forward and are associated with situational analysis, problem diagnosis, development and innovation. Developmental tasks represent the school's response to the need for change, which may be initiated within the school or stimulated by some external requirement. Contemporary examples of developmental tasks would be the establishment of a systematic and constructive system for monitoring the curriculum-in-action, developing parent-school partnerships, following up the recommendations of an OFSTED inspection, implementing a whole-school policy for teaching and learning, carrying out a post-Dearing review of the curriculum, or auditing the deployment of time within the school.

The core developmental task in a school is that of curriculum development and, alongside this, opportunities for appropriate staff development. Given the variation in subject knowledge/expertise it is unreasonable to assume that such important tasks are best carried out by individual subject-managers. It is much more likely to be undertaken successfully by a task group. A moment's reflection will remind us that in secondary schools a department or faculty head will carry out such work with and through a team devoted to the pursuit of a single subject and, even under such circumstances, it cannot be assumed that the process is unproblematic.

It is not always easy to achieve whole-school developmental tasks by means of a role culture. Rapid change and unpredictable demands are likely to put more weight upon a differentiated role model than it can bear. Job descriptions are soon outstripped by the need to engage in developmental tasks of a more pressing nature. Bailey (1992) has pointed out that job descriptions may outline 'idealistic rather than realistic definitions of responsibilities and workloads. The practice of listing all the desirable facets of a job without any reference to time allocation or levels of expectation in the performance of the various duties, inevitably places the conscientious job-holder in the "losers' corner": frequently the job cannot be done properly, however hard one tries'.

Some schools are beginning to adopt a mixed economy comprised of differentiated roles plus elements of a task culture (four such schools will be described in Chapter 4). Individual job descriptions reflect the essential *maintenance* tasks which are valued by all the members of staff on whose behalf they are undertaken. Task-focused project teams provide a complementary means of handling responsive-developmental initiatives of the kind outlined above. In medium to large primary schools, project teams will probably be made up of three to five teachers, though other staff may also participate when they have a particular contribution to make. Ideally, project teams would be led by individuals having particular skills or knowledge relating to the project at hand, but the nature of the developmental task may be such that no one has direct knowledge or experience in the area concerned. In those circumstances the team will be strengthened if some of its members possess generic skills such as a capacity to analyse, brainstorm ideas, think divergently, identify possible alternatives, and so on. It may be the case that some staff have had experience of action research and can bring this to bear.

Maintenance and development are relative terms. A developmental initiative in one school might well be subscribed under maintenance in another. Given this, it is useful for project teams to make a distinction between problems and puzzles. A problem has no ready-made solution and is best approached by a team whose members bring their analytical skills and ingenuity to bear. Puzzles, on the other hand, are dilemmas to which an answer already exists in the world. Many development tasks fall into the first category and in this situation a project team has many of the features of an action-research team. Others fall into the category of puzzles, in which case the team's time is better spent finding the solutions that exist elsewhere rather than in reinventing the wheel.

The essential conditions for effective project teams have been identified by West (1992b, p.74) as:

- commitment to the task;
- a clearly stated brief;
- agreed levels of delegated authority;
- adequate resources and service support;
- agreed ground rules;
- a feasible time scale;
- readjustment of existing workloads during the period of the project;
- agreed success criteria.

This mixed economy conserves energy, but for maximum effect needs to be located in a culture of extended collaboration. Its very nature reinforces the values that underpin such a culture and enables headteachers to set the pace of development at a realistic level. Once a team has completed a project, members revert to the individual maintenance functions outlined earlier.

---

### Activity 5

## MAINTENANCE AND DEVELOPMENT TASKS

- Review the tasks which you engage in as part of your job as a coordinator/subject manager, or equivalent role if you are a key stage coordinator. You may find it helpful to refer to your job description as you do so.

- List all the tasks which you have undertaken in the past 12 months in your role as a coordinator. Now make two lists in which you categorize the tasks in terms of maintenance or development.

- Look at the tasks which you have entered under the heading of development and consider whether a project team approach would have been a more effective means of achieving the outcome. You may, of course, have engaged informally with others in pursuit of some of them. This may be an indication of a collaborative culture at work and it may be a short step towards the mixed economy outlined in this chapter.

---

The 'mixed economy' approach has much to commend it. Small primary schools are essentially task cultures, unless they are managed by a headteacher who is hanging on to the role of indispensable heroic leader. The association of individualized tasks with maintenance goals and group tasks with developmental goals may be described as a matrix approach to management. Matrix management is a constructive means of ensuring that life in school is more manageable and that time is deployed to maximum effect. In a matrix approach the key questions for all staff to ask are:

- Are we clear about the goals we are seeking to achieve and aware of the goals of others?
- Are we clear on what goals this task is serving?
- Is this goal best achieved by an individual or by a team?
- Is this task one of the most important tasks that the school should be undertaking at this point?
- Are we making best use of time?
- Will this task benefit the pupils and if so, in what way(s)?

In such circumstances we should expect to find that *task descriptions and task briefs are as important as job descriptions*. Many members of staff are yearning to feel in control of their professional lives rather than feeling driven by external pressures originating from dirigiste government policy. They want to focus on promoting quality learning and are tired of requirements which distract them from this goal. One of the best ways of feeling in control is to predict the future and the best way of predicting the future is to invent it.

Chapter 3 will present a framework for whole-school development and indicates the role to be played by middle managers in the implementation of a policy for teaching and learning.

## OVERVIEW

It is important for middle managers to be aware of the characteristics of the culture of their school. Awareness of such features may help them to understand some of the problems which they encounter in the course of their work. A distinction between school cultures and management structures has been made. Three forms of collaborative culture have been outlined and the features of role and task cultures explored. It has been suggested that unless particular features are present, a differentiated role model may be difficult to achieve in a primary school. Within a task culture it is useful to distinguish between maintenance and developmental tasks. Subject development and associated staff development are best undertaken by task groups than by individual subject managers. A matrix approach to management has been outlined in which individual roles are associated with maintenance functions, and project teams provide the means of achieving developmental goals. Within a matrix approach task definitions and task briefs become as important as job descriptions and the latter are capable of being scaled down to manageable proportions.

*Chapter 3*

# A framework for curriculum development, policy implementation and monitoring quality

The purpose of this chapter is to present an over-arching framework derived from working with headteachers, assistant heads and coordinators , all of whom wished to explore constructive, manageable and feasible ways of responding to the requirements of the Education Reform Act. The purpose of the framework is to make the processes of curriculum development, implementation and monitoring more manageable. It is comprised of nine components, each of which is explored in the sections which follow.

Since the intention is to reduce complexity, it is useful to consider what types of documents are needed and their purpose. At present, many schools feel overwhelmed by the need to produce detailed documentation and are aware of the range of documentation which a school is invited to furnish prior to an OFSTED inspection, not the least of which are policy documents. All schools have policies of course, even if it is a policy not to have written policies, which is another way of saying that some schools have relied on implicit policy made up of shared assumptions and tacit understandings underpinned by custom and norms of practice. Such a stance may work effectively during times of stability but becomes highly problematic in times of turbulence and change. On the other hand, too many documents are more likely to confuse than clarify.

Most schools have a range of documents which reflect the priorities they have addressed over varying periods of time. In talking to coordinators it was clear that many were spending considerable amounts of time leading working groups charged with the task of producing draft policies relating to the curriculum. When policy documents were shared during 'policy swap shop' sessions it soon became evident that there were almost as many different ways of structuring a policy document as there were policies and that the term policy itself was subject to wide interpretation. There are very real dilemmas here: over-production of documentation by different individuals or groups may lead to overlap and repetition, a situation in which the production of the documents takes precedence over their purpose; too many policies produced in too short a time is likely to result in a massive implementation overload and token adoption; lack of conceptual clarity on what is meant by the term policy may lead to both ambiguity and over-lengthy documents; and the various policies, taken together, may lack overall coherence. Above all, there is the need to avoid 'paper fatigue', a situation in which staff are left enervated by a process which many teachers might claim is at best tangential to their 'real' job.

What follows is an attempt to provide a constructive response to the sort of dilemmas referred to above. The complete framework, comprised of nine components, is presented in Figure 3.1. It is offered as a conceptual framework to assist schools as they undertake the practical but complex and challenging business of improving the quality of teaching and learning. It is based on a few simple but effective management principles:

- wherever possible don't act until you are conceptually clear about what you are trying to do;
- keep things as simple as possible;
- wherever possible make one task do more than one thing;
- empower others;
- keep documentation action-orientated and avoid essay writing;
- make sure that everyone understands how the actions of individuals and the work of groups relate to the whole (hence the value of an over-arching framework);
- make sure that learning within the staff group is at least equal to, or greater than, the changes you are trying to bring about.

## COMPONENT 1: A GENERIC POLICY FOR TEACHING AND LEARNING

The first component in the framework is a policy for teaching and learning. Policy has been defined 'as a course or method of action *selected* (by an institution, a group or an individual) from among alternatives and in the light of *given conditions* to guide and determine present and future *decisions*' Webster's dictionary). There are three key words in this definition. First, the word *selected*, which implies that alternatives have been considered and that the policy will be less likely to be regarded as arbitrary. Policies are unique to given situations and we would therefore expect a school's policies to reflect its particular context and *given conditions*. The word *decision* reminds us that the major purpose of policy is to empower others. This definition is the more helpful since it does not trade in words which are sometimes regarded as synonymous with policy such as 'guideline', or 'framework'. This is not a semantic quibble. Within the framework described here specific meanings are attributed to such terms as 'scheme of work', 'guideline' and 'policy'.

Middle managers will be working within the context of a wide range of policies and it is therefore useful to make a distinction between two categories of policy: *generic* policy and *specific* policy. Generic policy focuses on a complex area of concern and in consequence is prone to a range of different interpretations. The central values which underpin the policy are likely to be contested. Examples of generic policies in the school context would be policies for teaching and learning, equal opportunities, staff development, or special needs. Desirable behaviour and principles may be outlined, but in implementing generic policy, staff are called upon to to exercise professional judgement. To use a theatrical analogy, the situation is akin to one in which staff share the same script and each is expected to enact a role creatively, but within the terms of the playwright's intentions. The fact that generic policies are susceptible to individual interpretation makes monitoring an essential feature of implementation. This point will be developed further as the framework is explained.

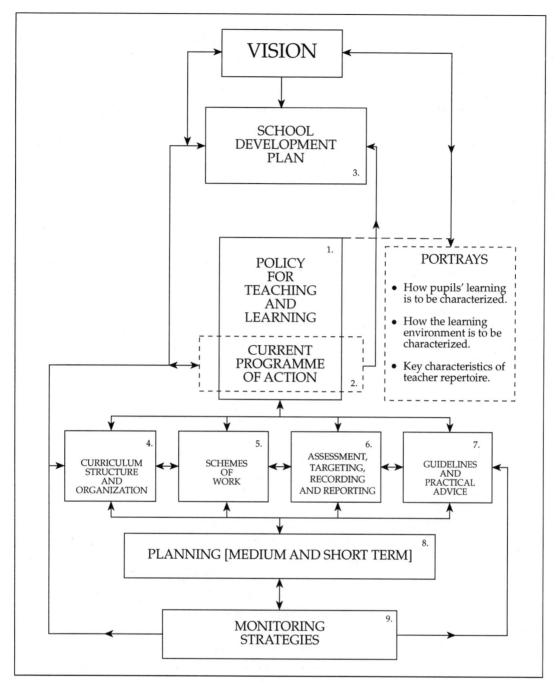

**Figure 3.1** Policy implementation and monitoring quality

The second category of policy, that of *specific* policy, embraces those policies which focus on much less complex areas of concern and which are much more amenable to codification or converting into protocol. Such policies link procedures to an agreed and intended result. Examples of specific policy in schools would be policies relating to school uniform, school visits, or finance and resource management. Since school governors will be involved in the process of policy formulation it is far preferable, in a situation where they may be unfamiliar with formulating policy, to work first on *specific* policy areas rather than expecting them to cut their teeth on a contested area of generic policy such as teaching and learning.

Policies represent the intentions or the 'oughts' of the institution and to this extent reflect the kind of place the school seeks to become. They represent a response to such questions as, 'Where are we now?', or 'Where do we want to be?' Some schools have responded to the second question by formulating a vision statement backed by policies which are congruent with that vision. Other schools have undertaken a strategic analysis of trends and needs and have formulated their policies in the light of such an analysis. Starrat (1990) recognized this distinction: 'Other educators are better engineers than rhetoricians. They will point to policies, structures and programmes in their school as embodying the vision of the school. To them it is the management arrangements that channel energy and attention towards those values and meanings that lie at the core of the school's vision.' In terms of the framework being offered here, a policy for teaching and learning lies at the heart of a school and is central to all that happens. The formulation of that generic policy will be the biggest investment a school makes on behalf of the pupils the staff seek to serve.

In the pre-ERA publication, *The Curriculum 5 to 16* (DES, 1985), HMI identified five characteristics of the curriculum that have gained wide acceptance within schools. The characteristics are as follows:

- *Breadth:* that is to say that the curriculum should bring pupils into contact with the eleven areas of learning and experience... (the National Curriculum presented these in terms of subjects, but the principle still holds true). To achieve this, HMI pointed out that teachers 'should be able to call on the support of teachers who, as well as having responsibilities for their own classes, act as consultants in particular subjects or areas of the curriculum. This is particularly effective when such consultants help other teachers to identify objectives, to plan the teaching and learning and to evaluate it' (para. 109).
- *Balance:* between the various areas of learning and experience, approaches to teaching and learning and forms of classroom organization.
- *Relevance:* 'in the sense that it is seen by pupils to meet their present and prospective needs...that all that pupils learn should be practical, and therefore relevant in ways that enable them to build on it or use it for their own purposes in everyday life' (paras 116 and 118).
- *Differentiation:* 'to allow for differences in the abilities and other characteristics of children, even of the same age...If it is to be effective, the curriculum must allow for differences' (para. 121, citing HMSO, 1980).
- *Progression and continuity:* in that learning experiences cumulatively lead to learning outcomes so as to 'ensure an orderly advance in their capabilities over a period of time...each successive element making appropriate demands and leading to better performance' (para. 121).

The question that these characteristics raise is the $64,000 question which every school must resolve through dialogue with coordinators and other members of staff, namely:

*What degree of variation in classroom practice is permissible if such criteria are to remain meaningful?*

A constructive answer to this question is to be found in a whole-school policy for teaching and learning The situation in the context of the National Curriculum may be summarized in terms of Figure 3.2.

Many schools have produced separate policies for each subject in the National Curriculum. Figure 3.2 proposes a *single* policy for teaching and learning which underpins the work in *all* the subjects. This strategy avoids repetition and simplifies the process of policy formulation. Instead of individual middle managers undertaking the same process (who needs nine generic policies?) we have the possibility of solving the problem by means of a task group comprised of the curriculum coordinators/subject managers led by the headteacher.

The rationale for this proposal is not based on organizational expediency: it is grounded in the view that the ways in which pupils acquire their sets of understanding in the different curriculum areas have more similarities than differences. As they participate in learning, pupils engage in investigative work, problem solving, hypothesizing, trialling, testing, exploring, communicating and so on; they acquire new concepts and extend existing conceptual frameworks, and they practise new skills and engage in their work through a mixed economy of individual, group and whole-class activities. The differences between subjects lie in the nature of the evidence that is cited in the different subjects and the tests for truth which are applied in the course of learning. The learning processes cited earlier are common to science, history, mathematics, drama, geography, art and so on, but the nature of the evidence is different in each case. The tests for truth that are applied in mathematics are peculiar to that subject and different from those which would be cited in, say,

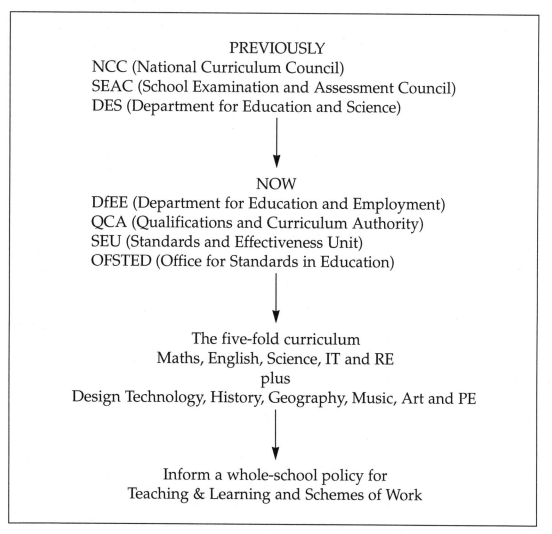

PREVIOUSLY
NCC (National Curriculum Council)
SEAC (School Examination and Assessment Council)
DES (Department for Education and Science)

NOW
DfEE (Department for Education and Employment)
QCA (Qualifications and Curriculum Authority)
SEU (Standards and Effectiveness Unit)
OFSTED (Office for Standards in Education)

The five-fold curriculum
Maths, English, Science, IT and RE
plus
Design Technology, History, Geography, Music, Art and PE

Inform a whole-school policy for
Teaching & Learning and Schemes of Work

**Figure 3.2**    A single policy, not one for each subject

history or music. This distinction was well argued by the educational philosopher Paul Hirst (1974) and many would say that the structure of the National Curriculum is largely based on his analysis of the nature of knowledge.

The policy for teaching and learning provides the answer to the question, 'What do we want to *witness* in classrooms'? a question which immediately evokes clear images of practice and helps to move us away from generalized principles and broad statements of philosophy which staff may affirm, but whose practice stays the same. The policy becomes the central reference point to guide the carefully sequenced work subsequently undertaken by middle managers. The policy is made up of three *elements,* each of which provides an answer to a specific question:

- *What should characterize the learning experiences offered to pupils?*
  i.e. What is it that we want pupils to do as they engage in the learning process? What is it that we should *witness* if we engaged in systematic observation over a reasonable amount of time? Clearly, not every process would be evident in every lesson.
- *What should characterize the learning environment?*
  i.e. What would we expect to see in the physical environment in terms of the management of teaching and learning resources, the layout and use of space, classroom organization and the ground rules which underpin the learning process? What does the learning milieu tell us about relationships between pupil and pupil, pupil and teacher?
- *What should be the major characteristics of the teacher's repertoire to achieve the high quality of learning experiences outlined in the first two elements above?*

## Formulating a policy for teaching and learning

Where coordinators engage in the formulation of individual policies for their subjects, the task has often been undertaken in relative isolation, with some consultation along the way with other members of staff. This approach has a number of problems associated with it. Policy documents written in isolation 'can become a source of mystification and a symbol of the remoteness and unreality of the school and its purposes. Policy is not encompassed simply by the old English art of essay writing' (Bailey, 1986). More importantly, a policy produced in isolation denies opportunities for others to learn. A policy for teaching and learning is best approached by a task group comprised of three to five curriculum and/or key stage coordinators with the headteacher acting as chair. Every member of staff will be involved in the process but at different times and with specific purposes in mind. All staff will have the opportunity to comment upon and add to drafts along the way. Governors will be consulted and kept informed.

The work of a policy working group may be outlined as follows. First, the group should analyse existing practice and draw together the ways in which learning is currently characterized in the school, the way learning environments are typified and the range of strategies currently used by the staff to promote learning. The task is one of descriptive analysis, not evaluation.

Second, in the light of the descriptive analysis the group should then identify what *should* be witnessed in respect of the three elements of the policy, and in doing so engage in dialogue with staff. This is likely to mean going beyond current practice and adding features which are essential if high quality provision is to be achieved.

The group may wish to invite outsiders with relevant knowledge and experience to help them at this stage. Where appropriate they may find it helpful to refer to the school's OFSTED or LEA inspection report together with published reports on schools similar to their own. Any and every relevant source should be explored. The criteria for inclusion in the policy is whether the point in question will result, in the long term, in benefits to teaching and learning within the school and not whether a particular point will be acceptable to everyone, or deemed too difficult to be attempted. Iconoclasm and the capacity to think divergently should be encouraged within the group.

Third, having identified the content of each of the three elements, the group should then make first drafts of each element and circulate these for comment to all teaching staff and to governors. Current concerns should be shared with governors during the process, not at the end. The purposes of the policy and its role in relation to the implementation of the National Curriculum should be explained and observations from the lay perspective welcomed. When consultations have been completed a first draft should be circulated to staff for comment and in similar fashion to the governing body. A final version should be approved formally by the teaching staff and the governing body.

Figures 3.3 and 3.4 give examples of content relating to the learning environment and pupil's learning experiences.

---

(Extract from a whole-school policy for teaching and learning)

The learning environment should be organized such as to enable:

- available space and materials to be used to best advantage;
- high standards of presentation and display;
- pupils to have ready access to learning resources;
- both independent and cooperative learning tasks;
- pupils to take an increasing role in the care and organization of learning resources;
- resources to be effectively displayed and stored;
- pupils to be aware that they live in a multi-cultural society;
- pupils to experience and enjoy an aesthetically pleasing context for their learning;
- pupils to take an increasing role in the mounting of displays of work which are effective and interactive;

...

---

**Figure 3.3**    Characteristics of the learning environment

### Definitions of teaching and the concept of teacher repertoire

The third element in a policy for teaching and learning is that of teacher repertoire. The concept of teacher repertoire was first developed by the author in 1986 and has been applied to a number of different contexts since that time (see, for example, West, 1992a and 1992b). The term has been found to be much more productive than teaching 'style' which is associated with simplistic dichotomies such as formal-informal; traditional-progressive; teacher centred-pupil centred, and the like. Teaching is being characterized here in the following ways:

- Teaching is construed here as intentional, which is to assume that the teacher intends to bring about learning of some kind.

(Extract from a whole-school policy for teaching and learning)

Pupils' learning experiences should be such as to enable them to:
- engage in problem solving and investigative work;
- apply concepts in new situations;
- communicate to others using a variety of media;
- gain first-hand experience;
- practise, apply and consolidate new skills;
- produce work for a variety of audiences;
- meet the challenge of completing tasks;
- use modern technology as an aid to learning;
- work individually and as members of a collaborative learning group;

  ...

**Figure 3.4**    Characteristics of pupils' learning experiences

- Teaching is regarded as both an art and a science. It is an art in the sense that teachers are responsive, intuitive, empathic, anticipative and engage proactively as they seek to meet the needs of their pupils. When we recall teachers who were significant to us in our formative years we often do so in terms of their artistry. Teaching is a science to the extent that certain aspects are susceptible to analysis and quantification. It is difficult to engage in shared analysis of teaching and learning if one of the partners in the process has the view that teaching is to be defined solely as one or the other.
- Teaching can be regarded as a series of planned, responsive encounters between teacher and pupil(s).
- If we extend the concept of teaching as a series of encounters still further, we can construe teaching as decision making. As teachers engage in teaching they are involved in making countless micro-decisions on the basis of information gathered as they scan the classroom, note pupils' responses, and decide to stay with their planned intentions or amend them in some way. Both the artistic and scientific dimensions to teaching inform such decisions. One way of defining quality would be in terms of the appropriateness of the decisions made by the teacher. It is not too fanciful to suggest that high quality teaching and learning often involve the teacher in taking some form of intellectual risk, i.e. actively experimenting with alternative strategies. Such teachers take a risk in order to 'know' more about what they do.

The process of repertoire construction begins in a formal way during initial teacher training and the opportunity for repertoire extension exists throughout a teacher's career. Many entrants will already have developed relevant sensitivities in the course of interactions of diverse kinds and draw upon these in making the decision to enter the profession. During initial training we move from 'threshold' or 'survival' repertoires to more extended forms of practice. The continuation of the process after training is dependent on the individual teacher's capacity to engage in critical self-reflection and explore aspects of their practice. Some teachers may be said to have had ten years' experience and others may have had one year's experience repeated ten times. It is possible therefore to locate a teacher's repertoire along a continuum with 'threshold' and 'extended' forms at opposite poles; this is shown diagrammatically in Figure 3.5. Repertoires are not fixed entities; they change

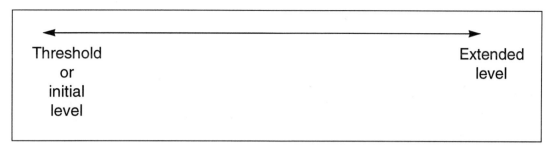

**Figure 3.5**    The teacher repertoire continuum

according to context. It is possible to have an extended repertoire in terms of English and also be located at 'threshold' level in terms of, say, technology. Repertoires are open to change and susceptible to changing requirements. The introduction of the National Curriculum had a temporary deskilling effect on many teachers. It is also the case that in the course of meeting new requirements many teachers have extended their repertoires considerably. Repertoire is therefore defined as:

the set of skills, devices, methods, strategies, knowledge and understandings which enables a teacher to make effective decisions in the course of promoting learning in the range of curriculum areas which they profess to teach.

Repertoire has proved to be a useful term of reference in the context of monitoring, since it enables us to proceed from a position in which no one has a 'perfect repertoire' and the idea of a preferred teaching style has been dispensed with. It acknowledges that learning is promoted through a wide range of skills and sensitivities such as lucid explanation, higher-order questioning skills, maintaining an effective classroom dynamic, the ability to engage pupils in effective forms of collaborative learning and so on. Effective teachers use a range of strategies ranging from whole-class teaching and the use of focused groups. Pilot projects on the use of the daily literacy hour have indicated the effectiveness of a balance between setting the learning objectives for the whole class followed by focused groupwork where the teacher works with one of the groups, concluding with a final whole class plenary session in which key points are brought out for the benefit of all pupils. The teacher works with each group in turn so that each receives 'quality time' aimed at improving standards.

In this, the third element in a policy for teaching and learning, the characteristics associated with the promotion of high quality learning are identified. These characteristics, like those relating to pupils' learning, or the learning environment, may be used as the focus for a programme of action.

The characteristics listed in Figure 3.6 are compatible with OFSTED's criteria for Teaching and Learning. These include sound knowledge, of subjects, high expectations of pupils, planning, methods and organisation, pupil management and the use of time and resources.

**Structuring the policy document and the question of length**

The final document might be structured as follows:
- a short outline of the origins of the policy;
- a statement of the aims of the policy and the needs which it seeks to meet;

This is an extract from the teacher repertoire element in a school's policy for teaching and learning.

Given below are the characteristics of teacher repertoire which we associate with high quality teaching and learning.
Each of them will be systematically and constructively monitored and explored in the course of successive whole-school action programmes. They are not presented in order of importance.

- effective and sensitive use of higher-order questioning techniques;
- clarity of exposition and explanation;
- design of challenging and differentiated learning tasks;
- focused teaching;
- positive rapport with pupils;
- ability to implement key characteristics of collaborative learning;
- effective use of learning resources including IT;
- effective and constructive management of pupil behaviour...

**Figure 3.6**    Teacher repertoire

- the three elements of the policy, each element being developed separately, and the various characteristics presented in bullet format;
- the resources which will be devoted to implementing the policy;
- review and evaluation, which outlines when and how this will be undertaken;
- appendices which can be attached to the document which outline

   a) the current action programme, and
   b) details of staff who are to play significant roles in the implementation/monitoring process.

An example of a policy for teaching and learning is given in Appendix 5 at the end of the book.

## COMPONENT 2: THE PROGRAMME OF ACTION

The programme of action is the second feature of the framework presented in Figure 3.1 and is the strategy used to facilitate policy implementation and monitoring. Policy formulation takes a good deal of energy and it is sometimes assumed that since staff have engaged fully in the process that they will, *ipso facto*, own the policy. That assumption confuses affirmation with the more important process of ownership and the latter can only be said to have occurred when the policy has been implemented.

One of the key functions of a subject manager outlined in Figure 1.2 in Chapter 1 was that of 'advice, documentation and support for staff'. One of the elements was that of policy implementation. It is not reasonable to assume that individual middle managers can undertake this role across the nine areas of the curriculum concurrently. If each coordinator, however hard working, engages in that process at individual level then what we may finish up with is atomized effort, tired staff, and no impact at whole-school level. Effective management is about working with and through others in order to maximize impact where it most benefits *all* pupils. It is about enabling things to happen, empowering colleagues and helping establish the necessary conditions. In Chapters 1 and 2 time pressures on middle managers were acknowledged and attention was drawn to the need to put such people in the winners' corner rather than creating overload. The suggestion was made that a mixed economy of task groups for developmental work and individualized roles for maintenance had much to commend it.

Implementing policy and monitoring quality are development tasks. A policy for teaching and learning is a generic policy, and as such it will be prone to a range of interpretations. Such a policy will outline aspects of teaching and learning which may not currently be part of normal practice at whole-school level. The policy represents the *'public map'* of intentions concerning practice. The policy will surface in classrooms where it reflects the *private image* of that policy as perceived by individual teachers. Some of those images will reflect inventive practice which none of the policy constructors envisaged at the outset. The purpose of coordinators engaging in the monitoring process as part of a programme of action at whole-school level is not to *prove,* but to *improve.* One way of doing this is to encourage inventiveness and creativity wherever it is witnessed or, as one HMI with a penchant for mixing his metaphors was heard to say recently, 'If ever you see a spark of creativity, water it!'

Teaching and learning is a complex process and it would be foolish to think that just because we have a written policy it is a simple matter for staff to adopt what it contains. The purpose of the programme of action is to facilitate implementation by taking *one* strand of the policy and making this the focus at whole-school level over a realistic period of time such as half a term. During that time the whole staff will delegate to a *group of coordinators* the joint tasks of implementation and monitoring. This argument will be developed more fully in Chapter 5.

## COMPONENT 3: THE SCHOOL DEVELOPMENT PLAN

In Figure 3.1 the link is made between the policy for teaching and learning, the programme of action and the school development plan. The business of implementing the most important policy in the school is of the highest priority. We should therefore expect to find the programmes of action lying at the heart of the school development plan.

## COMPONENT 4: CURRICULUM STRUCTURE AND ORGANIZATION

The policy for teaching and learning portrays what it is that we should witness as we observe the processes of teaching and learning. Such processes take place within a curriculum structure. The document on curriculum structure and organization represents the school's response to the Dearing Review (Dearing, 1993) and should make clear:

- the amount of time which is to be devoted to the different subjects or combinations of subjects. This can only be done by carrying out a careful analysis of the current use of time in the school day, week, term and year, questioning the outcomes and deciding on the best use of time. The DfE recommended a minimum teaching time of 21 hours per week at Key Stage 1 and 23.5 hours per week at Key Stage 2. In making decisions about time allocations due regard needs to be paid to the time taken up by registration requirements, collective worship and lunch and break periods and also to time which is taken up in the year on special events, school visits and by Key Stage assessments. From September 1998 all schools will be required to allocate a daily literacy hour and from September 1999 a daily numeracy hour will also be required

- how the different subjects comprising the curriculum are to be organized and the forms these should take in the various year-groups. It will indicate the subjects which are to comprise cross-curricular work such as topic, project or thematic work and which subjects are to be taught as separate entities. It will reflect due regard for balance within the curriculum. The guidance from SCAA, *Planning the Curriculum at Key Stages 1 and 2* (1995) refers to 'units of work' which fall into two broad categories: 'continuing' and 'blocked', both types drawing, in the first instance, on work from a single subject or aspect of the curriculum. 'Continuing work' is defined as 'a planned sequence of lessons or activities drawn from a single area of the curriculum' (p.40). 'Blocked' work can be taught within a specific amount of time, not exceeding a term. It should focus on a distinct and cohesive body of knowledge, understanding and skills. Such work can be taught on its own or be linked with units in other subjects or aspects of the curriculum. The requirement for schools to follow the KS1 and 2 programmes of study in the non-core curriculum subjects will be lifted until a revised National Curriculum is introduced from September 2000
- how decisions regarding curriculum structure have been agreed and the extent to which teachers' subject knowledge and resources have been borne in mind.

Awareness of the ground rules relating to curriculum structure and organization will greatly assist coordinators who have responsibility for drawing up the scheme of work in their particular curriculum area in consultation with their colleagues. The time allocations will be *indicative allocations* in the first instance and may need to be revised in the light of subsequent monitoring and evaluation. Component 4 of the framework should have the effect of safeguarding the entitlement curriculum of all pupils and assist coordinators when they make decisions relating to schemes of work. Schemes of work which cannot be fitted into the agreed curriculum structure are recipes for frustration.

## COMPONENT 5: SCHEMES OF WORK

Schemes of work are represented by component 5 of the framework shown in Figure 3.1 and provide a major focus for the work of the subject manager. In his 1998 annual report Her Majesty's Chief Inspector stated that 'about two fifths of primary schools lack effective schemes of work'. Schemes of work and the policy for teaching and learning might be described as the engines which drive the school forward. Schemes of work are not the same as policy and provide the answer to the question posed by every teacher who has a particular specialism but is obliged to teach eleven subjects, namely: 'What am I expected to teach to the age and stage of my pupils, in what sequence and with what degree of choice?' We need one policy for teaching and learning but we do need a separate scheme of work for each of the subjects.

### Types of scheme

There are three types of scheme of work.

*1. Central government initiated schemes*

These are schemes provided by central government which are the outcome of working parties comprised of teachers, advisers and the relevant specialists drawn from such bodies as the TTA, QCA and OFSTED. The Secretary of State at the 1998 NUT Easter conference stated: 'Optional ready-made schemes of work are being produced that will ensure that each year teachers do not have to "re-invent the wheel" as they prepare their schoolwork.' New schemes were introduced in the Summer term in science and information technology. Additional schemes in history, geography, and design and technology will come on stream at the time this book is published in the Autumn term of 1998. The national initiatives in Literacy and Numeracy should assist hard pressed subject leaders and provide useful resources which they need, particularly in small primary schools which do not have the full range of subject expertise. The launching of the Virtual Teacher Centre and Effectiveness Database on the National Grid for Learning (NGfL) provides a resource for subject leaders who wish to tailor national requirements to the particular setting of their school. The Secretary of State in April 1988 stated, 'These tools enable teachers to share ideas and good practice, to learn quickly from each other, and find out which schools are doing best and why.' The New Opportunities Fund allocated £230 million to supporting training for teachers in the curriculum use of information technology. The use of the Virtual Teacher Centre will be evaluated and published on the NGfL.

*2. School generated schemes of work*

These schemes have been produced by subject leaders or task groups of staff. The workload of subject managers in this aspect of their work has been prodigious. They have translated the programmes of study and QCA guidance into a form which is appropriate to the particular circumstances of the school (e.g. its multi-ethnic nature, the balance of SEN pupils or the characteristics of the catchment area). Subject leaders have worked with LEA advisers and have produced many schemes of work of the highest quality. The subject leaders concerned acquired an enormous amount of knowledge in the process and it is not surprising that a large number are now to be found in the ranks of the advisory services. Published OFSTED reports provide many illuminative citations of the work undertaken, sometimes in difficult circumstances.

*3. LEA derived schemes of work*

These are schemes prepared by working parties led by LEA advisers who have usually combined the construction of schemes of work with the preparation of strategies for assessment, recording and reporting which teachers have found of great value in their work. An excellent example of an LEA scheme is the Science Scheme of Work prepared by Hellen Ward of East Sussex Advisory, Inspection and Training Service. The Scheme, together with the Tasks for Science for KS1 are available from East Sussex Advisory and Training Services, at County Hall, St Anne's Crescent, Lewes BN7 1SG.

Subject leaders thus have three sources to draw upon when developing their schemes of work. It is quite proper that the schemes of work on offer are optional but schools must recognize that their performance will be judged on their ability to meet stated targets within an agreed timescale. It would be surprising if centrally produced schemes are very different from those produced by LEAs since many LEA representatives have served on the national pilot schemes. Schools will be held accountable for the quality of the schemes in use and it is this 'in use' aspect which is critical. Let us hope with Keats that 'Fine writing is next to fine doing, the top thing in the world'.

Where there is no scheme currently available for a certain curriculum area subject managers can learn a great deal by analysing those schemes which do exist. For each year-group a scheme of work should indicate to the teacher concerned:

- the content and key concepts to be taught;
- how the content is to be organized into appropriate units of work and how these are to be dispersed over the course of the year;
- how any interdisciplinary approaches might best be implemented, with clear examples and illustrations of the forms these might take;
- how the content is to be ordered and where choices might be exercised by individual members of staff;
- the time taken in teaching the various units, including the use of blocked time;
- what resources are available and where they are to be found.

The provision of effective schemes of work and a clear policy for teaching and learning should free subject managers wishing to devote more time to monitoring and evaluation. Chapters 4, 5, and 6 explore these in depth. 1999 should see a rapid expansion of the use of information and communication technology by subject leaders. They will shape the NGfL.

## SCHEMES OF WORK AND THE FUTURE

Given the rate at which knowledge expands and is subsequently made available, it is important that subject leaders systematically engage in the periodic review of their schemes of work. Subject leaders need to meet with colleagues to find out:

- how far the scheme of work is continuing to meet perceived needs;
- how far the scheme of work is continuing to assist staff when they engage in the detailed planning of their work;
- whether the scheme of work should be changed in any way.

## COMPONENT 6: ASSESSMENT, TARGETING, RECORDING AND REPORTING

Component 6 consists of the whole-school school policy for assessment, targeting, recording and reporting. Some schools have an assessment coordinator who has oversight of this part of the school's work whilst in others the subject leaders will work collectively on these areas. Some schools have found it preferable to have a separate assessment document rather than including agreed principles for assessment, recording and reporting in each scheme of work or in the policy for teaching and learning. The document should assist teachers by outlining what form assessment will take in the various subjects. It will also outline how, when and in what ways pupils' progress will be recorded and reported to parents, governors and recipient schools. The document should also indicate the role which pupils are to play in the assessment of their own work. Some schools have found various forms of pupil conferencing to be an economical and informative strategy to use. Moderation is a time consuming but invaluable learning situation for the staff involved and details should be provided on how, when and where it will take place.

The TTA has indicated that subject leaders have a clear role to play in analysing and interpreting performance data and in using such information to set realistic and challenging targets for improvement in their subject. In looking at SATs results or tests offered to schools by the QCA the schools should ask 'What do we do well? Are there elements in the curriculum that do not come up to expectation?' Scrutiny of marked scripts is a task for the subject leader who may find it useful to construct a matrix of pupils' names and test items. Scores can then be entered and analysis of scores will indicate areas of strength and weakness.

An understanding of level descriptors is important in the teaching of any subject. The programme of study details what should be taught and the level descriptors give an indication of pitch. This enables a teacher to plan work that is at an appropriate level of demand for the age group that they teach. Moderating that work with other members of staff at regular intervals helps to ensure that common understandings are maintained and that 'drift' does not occur. Teachers are susceptible to 'drift' where the results of a particular year-group are unusually high or low. In such a situation teacher expectations for the year-group may become distorted and in consequence inappropriate targets may be set. Where individual pupils or year-groups produce unusual scores it is important to seek explanations. Is it simply a random effect? Is it a consequence of poor teaching? Is it a consequence of the pace of teaching and learning being too fast or slow? Are the questioning and discussion techniques of staff up to the mark? A great deal can be learned from formative analysis of this kind. The most constructive stance to adopt in relation to testing and target setting is that of teachers as researchers. Assessment, formative evaluation and target setting provide an excellent opportunity for staff to work collaboratively on matters of direct concern to them.

Many LEAs are assisting schools by providing benchmarking data which enables subject leaders to compare their school with others of similar kind and size. Benchmark data should help to avoid complacency in schools which may have high ability intakes. It should also help schools where attainment levels are below par. It is important to go beyond the gathering and dissemination of performance data. What matters is what is done as a consequence of analysing such information. OFSTED inspection reports indicate that where a school has made formative use of performance data the quality of learning has risen.

SCAA (1997) suggested five questions which may assist the target setting cycle:

1. How well are we doing? (Subject managers will need to discuss and analyse performance data with heads and senior managers.)
2. (Here, subject managers are able to draw on benchmark data and PANDAS (Performance and Assessment Statistics) together with data from their LEA.) How well *should* we be doing?
3. What more should we aim to achieve this year?
4. What must we do to make it happen? (It is important to place targets in priority and balance the processes of pressure and support. See Chapters 4, 5 and 6 for useful strategies.)
5. The school takes action, reviews its success and starts the cycle again.

Many LEAs are publishing schemes of work in the core subjects together with materials and guideline documents which assist subject leaders in their work. East Sussex, for example, has published a range of materials of this type including one for Science in KS1 and 2. Recording formats are included and a supplementary document is specifically aimed at assisting subject managers in developing assessment in the areas of Experimental and Investigative Science. (*Science Scheme of Work* and *Tasks for KS1 and 2* are available from East Sussex Advisory, Inspection and Training Services, at County Hall, St Anne's Crescent, Lewes BN7 1SG.) The TTA has recently published needs assessment materials in literacy, mathematics and science for teachers at KS2. The materials have been extensively trialled and will prove useful resources for subject leaders.

## COMPONENT 7: GUIDELINES

Guidelines are neither policy, nor are they schemes. Their function is to service both in a specific way. Guidelines answer the question, 'How?' If, for example, a teacher has limited knowledge of science and is obliged to introduce pupils to the concept of mass, he or she might seek the help of the science coordinator. The coordinator is likely to respond to such requests informally, explaining what is needed, citing useful resources and so on. Where the same issue persistently recurs then the coordinator's response might be to mount a school-based workshop on the issue in question. But it is not always possible for every inquiry to be dealt with individually or by means of a staff workshop. Written guidelines fill this gap and are intended as a means of providing a first response to questions that have been raised. Over time an archive of such written guidance is established, an archive which may be of great assistance to new members of staff. Other examples of guidelines might be those relating to: collaborative groupwork and its organization; organizing an effective consultation evening for parents; the design of learning tasks; displaying the work of pupils; or the role of non-teaching assistants in the classroom. The inclusion of such detail in a policy document would make it unwieldy. Guidelines are akin to the sort of information which mountaineers might draw upon when planning how a particular feature on their route might be traversed.

## COMPONENT 8: MEDIUM- AND SHORT-TERM PLANNING

Medium-term planning is frequently undertaken within year-group teams supported by subject-managers or Key Stage coordinators. The planning unit is usually half-termly. Many schools set aside non-contact time for this type of planning. Schemes of work are transposed into detailed plans in which broad learning objectives are defined; resources are identified and allocated; confirmation is made of the way the curriculum is to be organized in terms of the agreed structures of different kinds of work and linkages; and assessment points are agreed. In terms of the overall framework, the role of medium- and short-term planning is absolutely crucial, since it is at this point that staff bear in mind the agreed focus for policy implementation and monitoring. The policy for teaching and learning has equal importance alongside the schemes of work. The planning should therefore make clear those aspects which constitute the developmental aspects of the year-group team. If, for example it had been agreed that the focus for monitoring during the half-term unit was to be collaborative learning, then it would be expected that each year-group team would provide specific details of this aspect in drawing up their plans. In drawing up their short-term (weekly) plans, each member of staff would outline how they intended to engage their pupils in collaborative groupwork, and what aspects of the latter they were seeking to extend as their contribution to the current programme of action (component 2 of the framework presented in Figure 3.1).

Medium- and short-term planning have to be kept in proportion. Most schools use some form of planning framework which provides a shorthand means of communicating current work across each year-group. What is being proposed here is a balance between shorthand frameworks and more detailed information in relation to the agreed monitoring focus for the half-term in question. This will be dealt with in more detail in Chapter 5.

The framework, comprised of nine components, each with a specific purpose, should inform the planning process and lighten the planning load. Where a specific time is set aside for planning, it is important for groups and individuals to check that Parkinson's Law is not in evidence ('Work expands to fill the time available'). It is important to ask these questions: 'Is the group becoming more efficient at the planning process?'; 'Do planning sessions start with a review of the outcomes of work completed?'; 'What was the standard of the pupils' work?'; 'Did it reach or exceed our expectations?'; 'On what evidence?' Planning sessions need an effective structure and it is the responsibility of the group to decide what form this might take.

## COMPONENT 9: MONITORING STRATEGIES

This is the final component of the framework and outlines the monitoring strategies which will be adopted in the school as the means of implementing the teaching and learning policy and monitoring quality. Examples of monitoring strategies are provided in Appendices 1, 2, 3, and 4.

This then is the over-arching framework which seeks to aid clarity and make the task of policy implementation and monitoring more manageable. It provides a map for middle managers to colonize by means of a mixed economy of task groups and designated maintenance/service functions. It is intended to provide the basis for half-termly programmes of action which are linked to the school development plan. Each programme of action is concerned with the implementation of policy in constructive, supportive but rigorous ways in which middle managers play a key role in realistic units of time. Monitoring as the strategy for policy implementation forms the subject of the next chapter.

## OVERVIEW

Each of the nine components in the framework has been defined and outlined. The central role to be played by a whole-school policy for teaching and learning has been emphasized and a distinction has been made between generic and specific policies. Policies, curriculum structure and organization, schemes of work and guidelines have been defined and the complementary function of each has been described. Middle managers have a key role to play in the formulation of a policy for teaching and learning and the construction of schemes of work and guidelines. In the light of the comments made by SCAA and the DfEE more attention needs to be paid to schemes of work. Such an emphasis fits well with the framework offered here. It has been proposed that policy construction is best undertaken by a task group and the stages in the process have been outlined. A distinction has been made between ownership and affirmation. Policy implementation has been presented as a complex process which needs careful management and which cannot realistically be achieved by individual subject managers working on their own. Guidelines offer specific guidance on matters of practice and complement policy. Planning should be informed by the various components comprising the framework and care should be taken to ensure that due regard is paid to the learning outcomes and standards achieved in previously planned units of work. Last, but not least, a whole-school policy for assessment, recording and reporting is needed which complements and informs practice in the various areas of the curriculum.

# PART II

# Making It Happen

*Chapter 4*

# From policy into practice:
# a question of quality

Previous chapters have outlined the dilemmas associated with middle management roles in primary schools. In Chapter 1 the origins of the scale post system were outlined and the feasibility of a differentiated role model of middle management was questioned. In Chapter 2 the cultural dimensions of schools were explored. An extensive literature on school improvement and school effectiveness suggests that the way forward lies in cultural change, in which schools, led by transformational leaders, are moved towards extended forms of collaboration in which the problems associated with intervention are largely ameliorated. Given the wide range of tasks and responsibilities placed on middle managers outlined in Figure 1.2, it was suggested that maintenance and developmental tasks be separated. Maintenance tasks would be linked to designated roles and developmental tasks to task groups as one way of reducing overload. In Chapter 3 the argument was taken one stage further and a framework outlined in which a policy for teaching and learning, curriculum structure, schemes of work, guidelines, and assessment informed the planning process. Sequential programmes of action were proposed as the means of achieving the joint goals of policy implementation and the monitoring of quality. If schools are to focus in depth on complex issues, such programmes need to be cast in feasible units of time. Half a term was suggested as realistic. This chapter will explore the monitoring process and go on to present practical strategies that middle managers might use in tracking policy into practice.

The literature abounds with accounts of coordinator practice illustrative of Kinder and Harland's (1991) observation that, 'the role that consistently emerged was one that carried a general, and very important, provisionary, informational and advocacy function rather than having any specific responsibility for individuals' practice' (p. 85). Coordinators/subject managers are often reluctant to take an interventionist stance on matters relating to classroom practice since to do so would violate social relationships. Rather than leaving middle managers to resolve this dilemma in their own particular way, what is being proposed here is that issues relating to implementation, monitoring and individual practice be addressed *corporately*. Instead of construing coordinator roles in terms of developing individual subjects, we need to move to the wider dimension of developing a school *through* coordination.

If the age of the heroic leader is over, so too is the image of coordinators as lonely missioners, each seeking to make a thousand flowers bloom in their particular curriculum garden. Most teachers came into the profession because they wanted to make something happen in a classroom. Like Lortie's (1975) teachers they reaffirm the 'central importance of psychic rewards, instructional goals, and evocative relationships.' Many such teachers now feel that they have been distracted from that key task by the successive demands placed on them since 1988. The framework described in Chapter 3 offers a means of putting teaching and learning at the top of the agenda and rekindling old sources of job satisfaction. Programmes of action will provide many developmental opportunities for middle managers, but not for all of them, all of the time. There is more than enough evidence which tells us that it won't work that way.

## POLICY IMPLEMENTATION AND MONITORING

The revised standards set by the TTA 'make clear that the degree to which subject leaders are involved in monitoring will be influenced by school policy and the size of school'. This correlates well with the six illustrations from schools of different size which are outlined in this chapter. Reference to the key purpose of subject leadership clearly indicates, that, size of school apart, 'subject leaders evaluate the effectiveness of teaching and learning, the subject curriculum and progress towards targets for pupils and staff to inform future priorities and targets for the subject'. Evaluation is a labour intensive activity and should not be engaged in for its own sake. The purpose of engaging in evaluation is not to prove but to improve. The sensitive collection of information should help subject leaders to identify effective practice and areas for improvement.

Monitoring is a sensitive issue, as reflected in the responses of over 300 coordinators to a questionnaire distributed by the author at the beginning of workshops. Less than 6 per cent engaged in any kind of classroom observation and of those who did, the practice was limited to either the induction of a newly qualified teacher or the context of staff appraisal. Fourteen per cent stated that they engaged in monitoring by sampling the work of pupils and that they subsequently discussed the issues which arose with their colleagues; 66 per cent reported that they did not currently engage in any form of observation or sampling of pupils' work. Kinder and Harland (1991) noted in their project that 'teachers also tended to interpret questions on monitoring as referring to a form of authoritative superveillance' (p. 193). That is not to suggest that monitoring is not going on. A good deal of valuable monitoring is, of course, already carried out by teachers, but it is usually informal and unsystematized and more often than not, taken for granted by them. In establishing overt, *corporate* systems of monitoring many schools have found it helpful to start the process from this 'naturalistic' end of the spectrum.

Monitoring answers the question, 'Do we do what we say that we do?' and is concerned with tracking policy into practice and improving practice in a constructive, supportive and rigorous way. It may be compared to taking a series of 'snapshots' or film clips of the curriculum-in-action and comparing these to the 'film script' of agreed intentions. It is about building quality in at the beginning and during the process, rather than relying on infrequent summative evaluations. Programmes of action provide the vehicle for *sustained* attention to *specific* aspects of teaching and learning. Such programmes recognize that teaching and learning are complex processes. In the course of monitoring we may come to understand a particular facet more profoundly, or even, perhaps, for the first time. To focus, say, on collaborative learning will require us to pose questions, go beneath the surface features of groupwork, analyse findings and explore the implications these may have in terms of current practice. In doing so, we will probably identify further questions along the way. Amongst the outcomes may be a firmer definition of collaborative learning, or an extension of teacher repertoires as a consequence of witnessing illuminative practice, or it may lead us to workshops on the design of collaborative learning tasks.

Monitoring is not something that is 'done' to colleagues: it is essentially a shared endeavour which is effectively managed at whole-school level. The rationale which underpins this approach to monitoring is given in Figure 4.1

In the course of policy implementation it is important to bear in mind the part that perception plays in shaping human behaviour. A policy for teaching and learning portrays what we wish to witness in classrooms and it is not assumed that such features are already in evidence or that everyone will interpret its constituent elements in the same way. One writer points out characteristics of perception in this way:

> There is a psychological mechanism in us which leads us to behave as if the world were the world as we perceive and understand it. The result of this mechanism is that we have the propensity to believe that what we know and do is 'right'. Intellectually, we can apply logic and acknowledge that the experience of others is different and that, like the blind man in the story, we have only got one perspective on the elephant of reality. But, emotionally, the force of this assumption is very strong. If our mental set remains fixed, then we will cease to learn significant things through our experience. (Manpower Services Commission, 1983)

As monitors, coordinators have to be aware of their own perceptions of the implementation process and alert to the predispositions of their colleagues. The following principles provide a useful *aide-mémoire:*

- Do not assume that because time has been spent in discussion and the policy for teaching and learning exists in written form that every member of staff will interpret it in the same way. Expect to find variations. Keep to the agreed focus and start from their assumptions, not yours.
- Give colleagues time to work through their meaning of the policy. Provide constructive analysis as a partner, not criticism.
- Recognize that policy implementation takes time. The programme of action in which you are acting as a monitor is a whole-school strategy. Be persistent but remember that Rome wasn't built in a day.
- Note inventive features of practice which no one identified when the policy was being prepared. Celebrate and disseminate such practice.
- Act as a catalyst for change and link colleagues who have ideas to pool.

Each programme of action focuses upon a particular feature of the school's teaching and learning policy. Year-group or key stage teams are required to pay particular attention to the agreed focus when planning their work in half-term units.

## THE MONITORING PROCESS: EXAMPLES FROM SCHOOLS

A case has been made for monitoring to be undertaken by task-teams rather than through the efforts of coordinators acting independently. The process needs to be underpinned by a rationale that is understood by all members of staff. The precise way in which monitoring is undertaken in individual schools will vary. Six illustrations of monitoring practice are outlined below which are based on descriptions of practice provided by schools. It will be noted that in each case headteachers and senior staff played a significant role in the process and endeavoured to involve and empower middle managers.

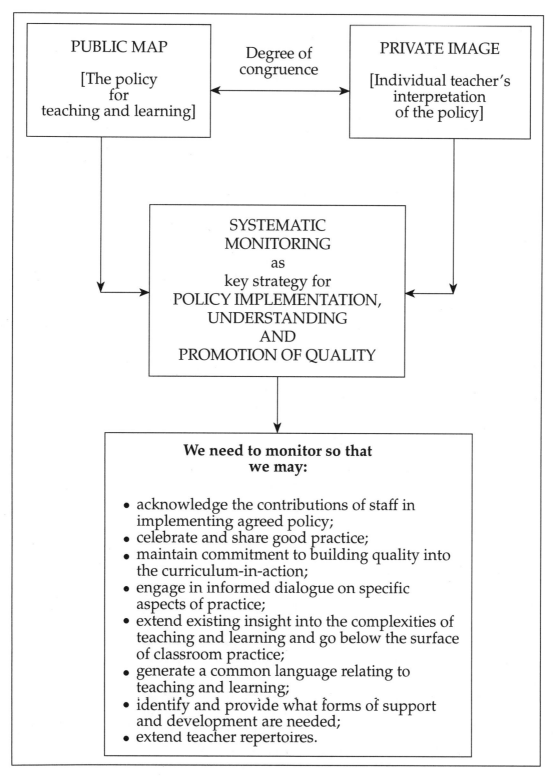

**Figure 4.1**   The rationale for monitoring

**School 'A' (a three-form entry junior school)**

Three key words might summarize the approach adopted in this school: initiate, monitor, and review. Three processes are undertaken in the course of each term:

a) the senior management team (head, deputy and two key stage coordinators) act as a pre-focus group whose purpose is to identify the focus for the following term and initiate discussion about the proposed aspect;

b) a monitoring group engages in monitoring the agreed focus identified in the previous term;

c) the senior management team follow up the implications which have arisen from the previous term's monitoring, which may take such forms as reviewing policy, the acquisition of additional resources for learning, or mounting school-based INSET sessions.

The monitoring group consists of the headteacher, or deputy, plus three curriculum coordinators. Other coordinators continue with their maintenance tasks. Membership of the monitoring group is based on knowledge and/or experience in relation to the agreed whole-school focus. Where such knowledge is limited, the group can still draw productively on criteria identified during the pre-focus stage. The work of all teachers is monitored including that of the members of the monitoring group. The group's task is to act as an agent for all members of staff, and members are responsible for managing individual feedback sessions as well as contributing to whole staff, key stage or year-group meetings. Decisions are then made concerning the need for additional exploration and/or support.

The resource implications per unit of 12 staff amount to three days' worth of release time per half term, representing an investment of approximately £2,000 per year. This sum would be supplemented by the school's current GEST (Grants for Education Support and Training) budget relating to the area of school effectiveness or from the school's staffing budget.

**School 'B' (small primary school with seven staff plus headteacher)**

In this school monitoring takes two forms:
a) the regular monitoring of cross sections of pupils' work in selected curriculum areas;

b) monitoring of the curriculum-in-action in which observers focus on the learning experiences of pupils.

The former has included, for example, pupil work associated with writing for different audiences; pupil work associated with recording investigations in science and mathematics; working models derived from problem solving in technology; and pupil portfolios produced in the course of topic work. The second form of monitoring is undertaken by the headteacher, deputy and/or relevant coordinator acting as a team. The non-contact time is facilitated by the headteacher who undertakes monitoring herself, and also covers for the deputy and coordinator when they do likewise. The headteacher devotes the equivalent of one day per week to the monitoring-implementation process. The staff have derived a good deal of satisfaction from this approach and feel that their work is valued. Planned development is closely linked to identified needs and the staff do not feel that the requirements of the policy are overwhelming them. In consequence the headteacher has a very strong sense of what is being achieved in the school and is encouraged by the way in which staff have been willing to be involved in the process.

The information collected during monitoring provides the bulk of the agenda for staff meetings and also informs INSET provision.

## School 'C' (urban JMI of 600+ pupils)

The school has an agreed policy for teaching and learning and has established task groups which are made up of staff drawn from every year-group in the school. There are four such groups, each associated with the following clusters of curriculum areas: science, maths and technology; the humanities (history, geography, RE and environmental studies); expressive arts (music, drama, art and PE); and language and communication (reading, language arts, and information technology). The core members of each group are the relevant coordinators to which are added other staff so as to make each group representative of all year-groups within the school. One member of the senior management team (head, deputy head, and two key stage coordinators) is allocated to each of the groups but does not act as chair.

The monitoring function is managed, a term at a time, by one of the curriculum cluster groups which selects the focus from the agreed teaching and learning policy or selected aspect of a particular scheme of work. Classroom observations are carried out by the member of the senior management team plus the coordinators from the curriculum cluster group concerned. During each term there are therefore two concurrent activities:

    a) the monitoring of a specific aspect in a cluster of associated curriculum areas by a curriculum cluster group;

    b) developmental work associated with the previous term's monitoring focus.

Release for monitoring is deployed in blocks of time with each monitor being released for the equivalent of three days' worth of time in the term in which they are acting as a monitor. The headteacher covers the class of the SMT member involved as a monitor. The approach has the advantage of limiting disruption to the classes of staff acting as monitors to one term in four, a factor that was appreciated by staff concerned. The monitoring strategy has been welcomed by staff who value regular feedback from colleagues who share the same range of constraints. Developmental initiatives arising from each monitoring unit are managed by project teams made up of colleagues who share the support/developmental role.

This method was more expensive to resource than school 'A', (approximately £4,500 per year) but this had been offset by savings made in the appointment of NQTs. (It has been calculated that the savings which can accrue from the appointment of NQTs who fill vacancies arising from staff turnover can amount to £5,000 per NQT [Levine, 1994]. Whilst a proportion of such savings goes towards the costs of inducting new staff, this still leaves a reasonable margin for use elsewhere, such as monitoring.)

## School 'D' (a 12 class infants' school)

This school has adopted a partnership approach to monitoring. Members of staff were asked to evaluate their own classrooms in terms of agreed criteria contained in the policy for teaching and learning or an aspect of a scheme of work. As a starting point, each member of staff identified the strengths and weaknesses of the ways in which they utilized space and promoted learning experiences of various kinds. They shared their perceptions with a self-selected partner and identified ideas for improvement. These ideas were shared with all the staff during a half-day closure. This resulted in a number of staff adding to or amending their initial ideas in the light of insights generated by the exchanges. Each partnership engaged in short observation sessions which focused on the change effort and explored outcomes based on mutual observation. Non-contact time was made available by a mixture of supply cover and headteacher release. A good deal of mutual exploration and explanation has taken place and the rate of inter-class visits has increased, a factor which will greatly assist subsequent monitoring initiatives at whole-school level

### School 'E' (JMI school, 250 pupils on roll)

This school has placed teacher repertoire at the centre of its monitoring strategy and each member of staff selects the subject/curriculum area which will form the context for classroom observation. Every member of staff has produced a repertoire profile (Figure 4.2 provides an example of one such profile) which indicates which subjects constitute their areas of strength and those in which they feel they have a less developed repertoire.

Three coordinators act as the monitoring group for a term at a time, after which membership changes. If, for example, repertoire relating to the promotion of collaborative group learning was the selected focus, each member of staff would decide on the subject area in which collaborative learning would be monitored in their classroom. When monitoring first began many staff selected curriculum areas in which they had extended repertoires but now, having established trust and seen the benefits, staff invite observations to be carried out in subject areas in which they know they have limitations. The variation in curriculum areas observed has not proved problematic since they are focusing on a specific aspect of repertoire irrespective of context. The coordinators acting as the monitoring group are expected to provide individual feedback and identify information which will be shared with the whole staff. The headteacher has decided not to be directly involved in classroom observation but is centrally concerned in the management of staff meetings based on shared observational data and also plays a central role in facilitating related developmental work. Coordinators not involved in a particular round of observations are expected to engage in the servicing and maintenance function in their non-teaching time. The costs here are approximately £800 per term.

### School 'F' (four teacher school, headteacher teaching 0.5, mixed-age classes)

It is not possible to release staff for observation given the constraints of the budget. Each member of staff has nominal responsibility for two curriculum areas. All the staff know the pupils well and operate as a closely knit team. Despite the resource constraints, staff felt that they could learn a good deal from monitoring. They undertake monitoring of the curriculum by exchanging classes for the equivalent of two half-sessions per half term, each teacher exchanging with a different colleague each time. An agreed whole-school focus is selected (for example, investigative science, creative writing, mathematics, topic work or an aspect of a scheme of work). Colleagues inform each other of the learning outcomes associated with a particular unit of work. Their task during the exchange period is to look at any relevant displays, examine a range of pupil work and, by talking with pupils in an open-ended way, gauge the levels of understanding displayed by the pupils in relation to the agreed focus. Pupils are invited to talk about how that engaged in their work, the key ideas they have explored and what they feel that they have learned. At the same time, points

A profile of an individual teacher is given below. It was produced following a workshop on teacher repertoire in which the term was explained and demonstrated. The profile is the response to the following question:

> If I were teaching these areas of the curriculum, to what extent can I, without undue preparation, provide and engage pupils in learning experiences of quality?

## COMPLETED PROFILE

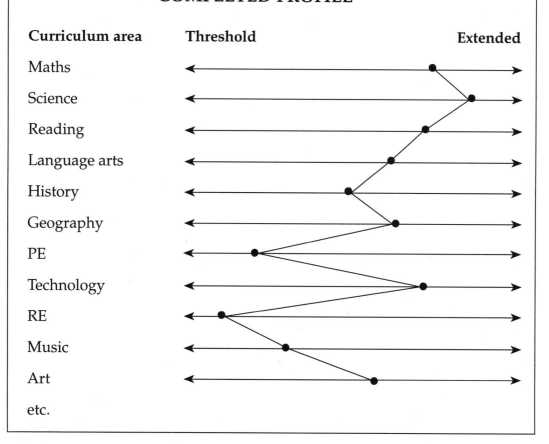

**Figure 4.2**   Teacher repertoire profile (For further information on repertoire, see West, 1992a; 1992b)

relating to curriculum continuity, progression and differentiation can be noted and here the staff have devised simple *aides mémoires* to assist them as they engage in this curriculum-centred enquiry work. Afterwards, staff meet together, share their findings and identify aspects for further exploration. The headteacher takes responsibility for organizing any support activities arising out of the data and agreed by the team. The staff enjoy keeping in touch with pupils across the age range. Knowing the staff well, pupils are very keen to talk about what they have been doing.

## MAKING A START ON MONITORING

Schools have started to introduce curriculum monitoring in a range of different ways. Some schools have first identified the range of benefits which should accrue to staff and pupils and have collectively mapped out what they feel to be the key purposes of monitoring. From there they have gone on to work out the rationale for the proposed system within the school. In doing so they have involved governors in their discussions and have valued the questions concerning quality raised from the lay perspective. But having done so, the practical business must begin. Some schools have implemented small-scale activities involving a single year-group. Others have first put the whole issue of monitoring quality on the agenda by engaging in a number of whole-school initiatives aimed at raising awareness. It is hoped that middle managers may find the following examples of 'starter' activities useful.

**Pupil track**

This is a useful activity which sensitizes staff to the issues relating to both the quality of provision and the process of classroom observation. Members of staff are offered the opportunity of working in pairs and engaging in the unobtrusive observation of a single pupil over a series of lessons. The focus is upon the pupil rather than the teacher, the purpose being to observe the experiences through the eyes of the pupil concerned. In leading workshops this proved to be a very productive preparatory activity in working with middle managers and with heads and their deputies. To avoid particular attention being given to the pupil in question, observers were asked not to divulge the identity of the pupil whom they were observing to the teacher concerned. Three questions are used as a simple observational frame:
  • What is helping the quality of pupil learning experiences?
  • What is hindering this?
  • What did the pupil learn?

**Focused self-evaluation**

Each year-group, with a coordinator acting as facilitator, engages in an evaluation of a recently completed and collectively planned unit of work. Each member of the group is asked to bring to the evaluation meeting their responses to the following questions:
  • What went well? (Identify specific information in support of your claim and be prepared to present this information to the group.)
  • Were there any aspects which you felt went less well? (As before, be prepared to provide information to support your response.)
  • Was all that was intended actually completed?
  • What is your assessment of the standard of work produced by a cross-section of pupils? (Bring a cross-sample of pupil's work and be prepared to cite these when

you present your account.)
- What did the pupils learn as a consequence of the unit of work? (On what evidence do you base your conclusions?)
- If you were repeating this unit of work, what changes would you wish to make?

In addition to the conclusions drawn, it is equally important to develop within the group the capacity to:
- provide *evidence* to support statements of different kinds;
- to disclose aspects of practice which are problematic to the individual concerned;
- to prepare for such sessions and take shared responsibility for learning within the group.

## Sampling pupil work

All schools are engaged in some form of moderation in relation to the assessment of pupil work and many do so during the selection of pupil work for inclusion in portfolios. Only 14 per cent of the questionnaire sample stated that they monitored through sampling pupil work from classes other than their own. A number of schools involved middle managers in joint planning sessions, when they offered advice in respect of their particular subject. An increasing number of key stage coordinators take in samples of pupil work and provide feedback to staff on key points noted across the sample. In doing so they are expected to bear in mind the learning objectives associated with the work and scan for issues relating to consistency and progression within and between classes. Many coordinators found this productive and they were able to make a number of observations which staff valued. The initiative needs to be based on a shared understanding of the purposes of sampling and the application of agreed criteria.

## Conversing with pupils

Staff are asked to work in pairs with a self-selected partner who may or may not be from the same year-group. Each teacher shares with a partner the intended learning outcomes of work they have recently completed with their pupils. They also identify a small number of pupils across the ability range who will be key respondents. Having done so, the teachers exchange classes for approximately half an hour. They engage in dialogue with pupils, drawing in key respondents, and use the following framework of questions, transposed into appropriate language for the age-group concerned:
- Tell me about this work (referring here to the agreed topic or subject and the work itself, which might be in an exercise book, a folder or mounted in some form of display, etc.)
- How did you go about the work?
- What do you think were the key ideas?
- What do think you might learn next in this subject/topic?
- How might you go about doing that?
- How long do you think it would take you?

The purpose of the approach is not to catch pupils out, or to measure the outcomes of the work at hand. The purpose is to explore and extend pupils' capacity to talk about their work, to conjecture about what might follow from what they are currently engaged in, to suggest how they might do so (In groups? Individually? As a whole class?) and the reasons for their suggestions. This is a relatively unthreatening but focused way of entering into productive dialogue on current work. It raises awareness of the value of communicating learning objectives to pupils, getting them to reflect on their work and consider what might then follow.

### Pupil expositions

Here pupils from classes which have undertaken the same topic or theme join together to share what they have learned. This is sometimes done in a large forum or in smaller groups where this is felt to be more appropriate. Pupils explain to each other how they went about the various learning tasks, what they found particularly interesting or challenging, and any aspects about which they remain unsure. The pupils need time to prepare what they have to say and care needs to be taken to avoid dominant behaviour by more articulate pupils. The staff involved manage the session or facilitate a small group but its central characteristic is that of pupils talking to pupils with the staff actively listening to the dialogue. It will only be effective if pupils feel that what they have to say is valued by their peers and by their teachers.

### Sharing learning environments

This approach has been found helpful in schools where there is anxiety about the prospect of classroom observation and there is no tradition of shared practice. Over a period of half a term, each member of staff is asked, in turn, to present a commentary on the organizational features of their classroom and how space and resources are used to support different kinds of learning, referring as they do so to current examples evident in the classroom. The commentary is presented in the classroom of the teacher concerned. Some schools have called successive staff meetings in different classrooms of the school, each meeting being preceded by an account from the host teacher.

### Laboratory lessons

Advantage is taken of a day or half-day closure for staff to witness and monitor a lesson taken by a coordinator. The lesson is presented as an opportunity for staff to collectively engage in constructive, focused observation of an agreed aspect which is currently being explored within the school. Examples of the latter might be higher-order questioning techniques, or investigatory work in mathematics, or problem solving in drama, or the application of a concept to a different context. Such lessons are not presented as ideal practice but as an instance of practice for the purpose of exploration.

## THE ISSUE OF SUBJECT/CURRICULUM DEVELOPMENT

It seems reasonable to locate responsibility for subject development in secondary schools to specific subject departments or faculties which are largely staffed by graduates in the subjects concerned. The structure of departments and faculties is reflected in specific roles such as head of department/faculty together with posts which are allocated points above the SNS. The challenge of subject development can thus be spread amongst members of the department. In primary schools we cannot assume that staff who have designated responsibility for a specific subject are graduates in that subject, or even that it formed their main subject in their college years. This is an issue outside the control of schools: it is one which relates to the supply of teachers and the characteristics of the pool of available teachers within an LEA. It would be an unusual primary school which had each of the eleven subject areas led by a teacher who was appropriately certificated. How then are primary schools to effectively manage subject development and what is the role to be played by coordinators?

Where there is serious shortfall in subject expertise, schools may choose to buy in the services of LEA advisers/inspectors, or they may consult with colleagues in the relevant department(s) of the recipient secondary school. They may decide to draw upon expertise in other primary schools within the locality. They may decide to invest in further training of particular members of staff. They may do any or all of these things. An additional response to the problem may be to draw upon the the same project teams which undertake policy-related observation and feedback.

The need for development within a specific subject area may have been identified in the course of policy-related monitoring, but it may also stem from developments identified by subject associations, or as a result of research, or as a consequence of recommendations from SCAA, OFSTED or QCA. The weight of subject development is more productively borne by project teams than by colleagues who are willing but not particularly knowledgeable in the area concerned. Most medium-sized primary schools would be able to provide one subject certificated and/or experienced teacher(s) within such clusters as maths and science; reading, language arts and information technology; humanities (history, geography and environmental studies); and the expressive arts (music, drama, art and PE). The goals of such teams would be to promote learning within the group and take the lead in relevant curriculum development initiatives. No single team would be expected to be involved concurrently in observation and curriculum development activities. This mixed economy of designated roles for maintenance purposes and task teams for developmental initiatives fits well with the responsive, sharing, reciprocal culture of primary schools.


## OVERVIEW

This chapter has explored the monitoring process and presented this in terms a corporate activity undertaken by a group of middle managers and managed by the headteacher or the senior management team. Monitoring is concerned with tracking policy into practice and improving practice in a constructive, supportive and rigorous way. It is about building in quality during practice rather than relying on piecemeal feedback or infrequent summative evaluations or inspections. A rationale for monitoring has been presented (Figure 4.1). Middle managers need to be aware of the role played by perception in shaping the expectations of others and to be alert to the pre-dispositions of their colleagues. A set of principles has been offered which may be found helpful. Six illustrations of monitoring practice have been outlined together with seven starter activities which schools have used to sensitize staff to some of the issues relating to monitoring.

In discussing issues relating to monitoring, attention has been paid to its nature and purpose and examples have been provided of different ways in which schools have structured the process. An emphasis has been placed on the part to be played by observation since the three key elements in a policy for teaching and learning portray what it is that we should witness in classrooms and, by implication, what the school is systematically trying to develop.

The issue of subject development has been addressed and it has been proposed that this is best undertaken by project teams rather than individual subject-managers.

*Chapter 5*

# Policy-related observation and the implementation of schemes of work

This chapter explores issues relating to observing the curriculum-in-action and focuses on process skills required by middle managers undertaking monitoring in their school as members of a monitoring group. Monitoring and policy implementation are regarded here as developmental activities best undertaken by a task team of middle managers acting as agents on behalf of the group rather than by individual subject-managers with all the associated problems relating to intervention. Acting as an agent on behalf of colleagues may seem a somewhat daunting prospect, but such feelings may be lessened if the purposes of policy-related observation have been shared with staff and opportunities have been provided for everyone to raise questions and express their concerns. Coordinators are also likely to have anxieties and points they wish to raise in staff discussions. Middle managers are, after all, fellow colleagues who share the same concerns as everyone else. This formative stage should not be hurried.

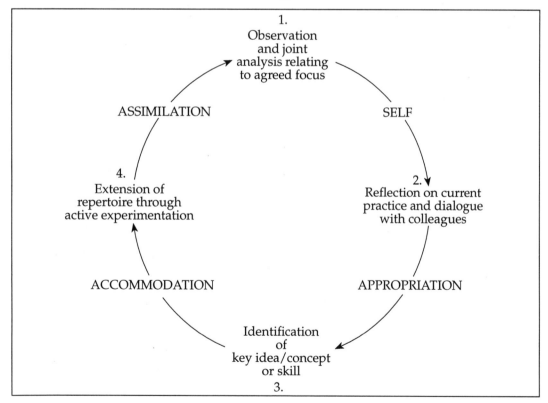

**Figure 5.1**   The monitoring-feedback process

Policy-related observation is essentially a developmental process which draws on the experience and insights of co-professionals who are willing to facilitate and promote individual *and* institutional development. Observation provides the basis for sustained and informed dialogue at whole-school level on an agreed focus. Monitoring assumes a relationship between feedback and development and is predicated on the assumption that staff are willing to take responsibility for their own learning. Constructive focusing on a specific aspect of practice should foster the kind of persistent dialogue that can act as a spur to individual experiment.

The process can be represented in terms of the cycle shown in Figure 5.1. Observation is undertaken in relation to an agreed whole-school focus, followed by feedback involving the joint analysis of data(1); the teacher reflects on the monitoring experience and considers current practice in the light of dialogue which is being promoted at whole-school level (2). The third step is the most important, for here the teacher goes beyond the observational data, takes responsibility for his or her own learning and in doing so, identifies and explores key ideas, concepts, or alternative strategies (3). The latter are then incorporated into their repertoire through active experimentation, reflection and ongoing dialogue with colleagues (4).

In paying attention to individual development we should not lose sight of the importance of institutional development. If the outcomes of the various observations are not brought into productive relationship it will not be possible to refer to policy implementation or the implementation of schemes of work in a rigorous way and the opportunity for institutional learning will be diminished. This takes time and is another reason why monitoring needs to focus on a particular aspect in units of at least half a term. It is useful to construe institutional learning as *team-learning*. The essence of team learning is dialogue. The Greek term *dia-logos* meant a free-flowing of meaning through a group, a process which allowed the group to discover insights not attainable individually. Senge (1990) suggests that the practice of dialogue has been almost completely lost to modern society but notes that, 'Today, the principles and practice of dialogue are being rediscovered and put into a contemporary context. (Dialogue differs from the more common "discussion", which has its roots with "percussion" and "concussion", literally a heaving of ideas back and forth in a winner-takes-all competition)' (p.10). The team-learning dimension to monitoring needs to be safeguarded and thought should be given as to how whole-staff sessions might be managed productively. There may be members of staff who have particular skills in promoting *dialogue* rather than discussion. If so, their services will be invaluable.

The previous chapter outlined ways in which systematic monitoring might be introduced by building upon informal or 'naturalistic' practices, followed by the adoption of an appropriate form of organizational structure. One way of developing insights into classroom observation is for prospective observers to engage in systematic observation in their own classrooms. Three activities found useful by coordinators in preparing themselves for the role of observer are outlined below.

## OBSERVATION: MAKING A START

### In your own classroom

The best place for a potential observer to start is in the context of their own classroom through self-conscious attention to a self-selected aspect of their classroom practice. The rule here is to 'act small but think big'.

## Activity 6

## MAKING A START IN YOUR OWN CLASSROOM

You already engage in a good deal of informal monitoring in your classroom. In the course of your work you scan the classroom, note pupils responses, listen to them, talk with them, examine their work and in consequence make decisions about how to proceed and in what ways. The purpose of this activity is to raise awareness of key issues that need to be addressed when establishing policy-related observation. Answer the following questions as fully as you can:

- *Why* do you wish to engage in a more systematic approach to observation in your classroom? What benefits might accrue?
- *What* or *Whom* will you select as the focus of your observation? When you engage in monitoring you will be focusing on a particular facet of the policy for teaching and learning, but for now, choose an aspect of pupil behaviour that will be amenable to systematic observation by you as you teach the class. You may wish to select a particular pupil and focus on one of the following aspects:
  - time on task, time off task, and task-related behaviour;
  - verbal interaction with fellow pupils during groupwork;
  - verbal interaction with you during a lesson.
- *When* are you going to undertake the observation? During which part or parts of which lesson(s)? Given that you have ongoing responsibility for the class, what might be the most appropriate timing of your observations given the focus you have selected?
- *How* are you going to observe, and how will you record your observations? Do you intend to use an observational framework of some kind? If you do, try to keep it as simple as possible. If you decide just to make notes you may find it helpful to separate judgements from descriptive data by making two columns on a sheet of A4, one headed 'Judgements' and the other 'Description.'

When you have completed your observation, try to expand your notes as soon afterwards as possible. When you have done so, pose the following questions against the information you have collected:

- What is the information 'telling' you?
- How might you substantiate any inferences that you have made?
- What implications follow from your interpretation of the data?
- What questions about classroom observation has the experience raised for you?

---

## Activity 7

## REFLECTION ON TEACHING AND LEARNING

The Open University's Curriculum in Action (OU, 1980) uses six questions about the curriculum-in-action which provide a useful framework for teachers to use when reflecting on teaching and learning. They are:

1. What did the pupils actually do?
2. What were they learning?
3. How worthwhile was it?
4. What did I do?
5. What did I learn?
6. What do I intend to do now?

Apply the questions to a particular lesson or activity. Questions 1 and 4 require you to construct a descriptive account of what took place. Question 2 operates at two levels: at the simplest level we can state what it was that we intended the pupils to learn, but in order to know what they have learned it will be necessary to talk with the pupils. Question 3 raises the issue of judgement and what criteria are to be used in defining worthwhileness. Question 5 requires you to analyse the data you have collected and reflect on the conclusions you have drawn. Question 6 invites you to take action in the light of your analysis.

If possible, work with a colleague who is using the same framework to their work. Share your findings. What issues has the activity raised in relation to observing in classrooms other than your own?

**TALKING WITH PUPILS**

Policy-related observation will involve you in the collection of information relating to the quality of learning experiences offered to pupils. As observers we have no way of knowing the pupils' perceptions of the work at hand. As observers we can only make judgements based on the surface behaviour that we witness and these need to be checked out by talking with pupils. We cannot realistically expect to talk with every pupil in the class but it is usually possible to talk to a small sample. This activity will require you to check out the inferences that you may make in the course of analysing information. As before, you may find it helpful to undertake the activity in parallel with a colleague and share the issues which arise.

Make a simple plan of your teaching space with squares to represent the boys and circles for the girls. During a discussion period, put ticks to indicate which pupils make verbal contributions. Examine the subsequent record and construct the following categories:

- Pupils who made no verbal contribution in the course of discussion.
- Pupils who contributed of their own volition.
- Pupils who made contributions but only as a consequence of some action on your part.
- The number of contributions made by a) different boys, b) different girls.

What inferences do you draw from looking at the pattern of contributions?
Are there any surprises?
Check out your inferences by talking with some of the pupils concerned. As you do so, guard against using leading questions.
Are there any alternative inferences that could be made?

# THEORIES-IN-USE

Argyris and Schon's (1974) theory of professional learning provides an illuminative framework in the context of policy-related observation since we are particularly interested in the match between the intentions outlined in the policy or the schemes of work and particular features of practice. They suggest that as we engage in our work, we use what are termed our 'theories of action ' and that all theories of action take the same form, namely, 'in situation S, if you want to achieve consequence C, under assumptions a(1)…to a(n) do A'. We use a wide range of such theories of action when we teach, and these interrelated theories of action make up our theory of practice. If, however, we ask someone to tell us their theory of action in a particular context (e.g., how do you teach history to your class?), what the person relates to us is their *espoused theory of action* for that situation. This is the theory to which they give their allegiance and which they communicate to others when asked about their intentions. However, what governs action is a person's *theory-in-use*, (what they actually do), which may or may not be congruent with their espoused theory of action. We cannot learn someone's theory-in-use just by asking them; we have to construct their theory-in-use from observations of their behaviour. The implications of this for classroom observation are considerable, not least because the less we know about the antecedents to a lesson the more we will be 'free' to construct the person's theory-in-use by making inferences from the behaviour we observe. Here is an example of how this approach was used with a teacher in a Year 4 classroom.

The teacher was asked to typify how she went about teaching history to her pupils (her espoused theory of action) and was asked to write this down and place it in a sealed envelope. She was then observed as she taught history. The observer carefully noted the characteristics of the teacher's practice as she taught a history lesson: what she did to promote learning, what she got pupils to do, the questions that she posed, the way in which the learning was organized, the concepts that were being explored, and the attitudes being fostered, in so far as any of these were evident in the course of the lesson.

The observer's task was to construct a descriptive analysis of what was happening rather than to make value judgements on what was being observed. After the lesson the teacher was asked to reflect on what had happened and make notes on her perceptions of the lesson, constructing, from her perspective, a descriptive account of what had taken place. The next day the teacher and observer met for the feedback session. The teacher was first asked to present her perceptions of the lesson. The observer then presented his description of her theory-in-use, highlighting the salient characteristics and citing descriptive evidence to support the statements made. Having done so the observer then opened the envelope and read the teacher's espoused theory of action relating to history. The teacher's espoused theory read as follows:

> I am not a historian, I trained in science and have a commitment to learning from first-hand experience. History uses many of the processes associated with scientific enquiry. What differs is the nature of the evidence and the tests for truth that one applies to such evidence. Historical processes consist of looking at evidence, hypothesising and making some sort of conditional statement. It is important to test these through discussion and to encourage pupils to subject their conclusions to the scrutiny of others. What matters at this stage with my pupils is that they engage in observation, get some idea of the concept of change, talk about what they think, listen to the contributions of others, make hypotheses, develop these and test them with their peers, and finally record them in some form. My job is to pose questions and listen to their answers and to foster positive attitudes to history. It may be possible to verify the conclusions that have been made by referring to the work of professional archeologists or historians.

This statement was then used as the reference point in the exploration of consistencies and inconsistencies between intentions and practice. In this particular case there was a high degree of congruence between the teacher's espoused theory-of-action and her theory-in-use. There was ample evidence that pupils had engaged in formulating hypotheses and had then gone on to make statements about what they thought the objects were. There was strong evidence of pupils presenting accounts to their peers and actively listening to each other. Where pupils felt unable to reach a conclusion they said as much, and did not try to invent reasons for the sake of doing so. If they did not know, they said so. Conditional statements such as, 'I think that this object is probably…'; 'It's because…'; 'It might however…'; 'You can't say that because…' were in evidence in each of the 'curator groups', which was the strategy used to manage the lesson. Each group had different pictures to explore since the teacher had no access to historical artefacts on this occasion. The feedback session had a strong evidential base and led to very productive discussion on a number of points:

- How the ground rules for this kind of work had been established and how they might be drawn upon still further.
- What might constitute other approaches to the teaching of history and why.
- How far pupils of this age were able to interpret visual images of real objects in comparison to handling actual objects.
- How pupils of this age might engage in the business of validating their hypotheses.
- The importance of higher-order questioning in this approach and how such skills might be extended.
- The issue of pupil's tautological thinking, e.g. Teacher: 'Why do you think that might have been a candle holder?' Pupil: 'Because it looks like a candle holder.'

- The formats used by pupils to record their findings.

The pupils had in fact, been looking at pictures of artefacts relating to the Sutton Hoo treasure ship, but they had not been told this. Their job was to try and make sense of the evidence that they had been given. At the close of the project, the teacher showed the class videos of two TV programmes which outlined what archeologists had discovered about the Anglo-Saxons from the evidence found at the Sutton Hoo site. The interest level of the pupils was very high. They wanted to know if their conjectures were accurate. Many children were delighted to find that what they had thought had been validated but, as one boy said at the time, 'That's true at the moment, but somebody else might find out something different'.

Kurt Lewin (1935) observed that there is 'nothing so practical as a good theory.' Theories of action are useful tools to colleagues seeking to illuminate the complexities of classroom practice.

---

**Activity 9**

**USE OF VIDEO**

The video camera can be used to good effect as a tool to promote self-reflection and raise awareness about aspects of observation. The following activity provides some suggestions for those wishing to use such a resource.

Use of the video camera is a common event in the lives of many pupils. Even so, it is important to allow pupils time to get accustomed to the presence of a tripod-mounted camera in the classroom, to handle the camera and see themselves on tape. Lock the viewfinder on to the space that you will be using during the selected lesson or activity. Choose a subject area which is at the extended end of your repertoire and write down how you would typify your practice in that subject. Video yourself in action, analyse the video and reflect on the degree of congruence between your actual practice and what you espouse. Make notes on specific aspects which you would like to explore more fully and use the camera again as an observational tool.

---

## MUTUAL FORMS OF CLASSROOM OBSERVATION

Practising classroom observation need not involve the observation of complete lessons. Many useful insights can be gained from ten or 15 minutes' worth of observation in a colleague's classroom. If you can engage in mutual observation with another middle manager who will be a member of the monitoring-implementation team, that is even better. Remember that the purpose is to gain insights into the processes of observation and feedback. If the colleague has a specific aspect on which he/she would welcome feedback then take the opportunity offered, but make sure that the focus is a realistic one in the short periods of practice time envisaged here. You might for example focus on such aspects as:
- the first ten minutes of the lesson, focusing on how the work was initiated and the nature of the pupils' response;
- the final ten minutes of a lesson, focusing on pupils' task-related behaviour;
- a particular group of pupils during groupwork, focusing on pupil-pupil interaction;
- the content of teacher-talk;
- teacher questions;
- talking to pupils about their work using an agenda set by your colleague;
- pupils' use of learning resources.

# KEY POINTS WHEN UNDERTAKING POLICY-RELATED OBSERVATION

When prospective observers have gained initial insight into the processes of classroom observation, they can then undertake observations for longer periods in classrooms other than their own. This might then be followed by a small pilot in a limited number of classrooms in which observations have a common focus of the kind envisaged in policy-related observation.

The time span for a single programme of action will be at least half a term. Within that period there will be a common focus taken from one of the three elements which make up the policy for teaching and learning or from one of the schemes of work. The purpose of the monitoring is to assist implementation and provide feedback on the quality of learning experiences offered to pupils. If, for example, the selected focus was that of collaborative learning, the following aspects might be discussed with staff prior to the programme of action as a means of raising awareness of dimensions to such work:

- findings related to collaborative learning from such sources as Galton, 1980, 1995; Johnson and Johnson, 1975; Kutnick, 1988; Slavin 1983;
- the degree to which the learning task(s) required, and thus promoted, inter-dependency for the achievement of the learning goals;
- evidence of pupils' understanding of the ground rules underpinning collaborative work;
- differences between helpfulness and collaboration;
- pupil participation rates within a specified group;
- evidence that pupils understood what was expected of them;
- the standards of pupils' work;
- teacher-group interaction;
- teacher-pupil interaction.

It would be very difficult to focus on all of such aspects in the course of any one lesson. Much will depend on individual teacher's repertoires in relation to collaborative learning. The precise focus will be agreed between the two partners concerned. The mutual goal is to add to existing knowledge and insights on the nature of collaborative learning.

An agreed rationale for monitoring should produce a situation in which colleagues genuinely want to receive feedback on their work and are prepared to experiment and take a risk in the course of their teaching. The process has many of the features of action-research. In this situation, if you have sufficient trust in your observer-monitor to self-consciously attempt to extend your skills in the agreed aspect, the outcomes of the monitoring process will be productive irrespective of the relative 'success' of the lesson. If you simply play safe then the opportunity to extend your repertoires is very limited.

When implementing this kind of systematic monitoring it is useful to bear the following points in mind:

1. The parties should have a clear idea of what constitutes the focus for the observation.
2. The observer is acting as the agent of the colleague who is being observed.
3. Monitoring is an expression of partnership between co-professionals.
4. The partners need to take joint responsibility for the construction of observational frameworks which might be used. The school will be able to build up a bank of such frameworks for use by others.

5. The partners should decide on whether the observer is to be a non-participant or participant observer and the reasons for that decision. They should identify any pupils whom the observer might talk to in the course of, or at the end of, the lesson.

6. Decide on how the observer will be introduced to the class. The following form of words has been found helpful: 'Mr/Ms X is spending time with us this morning in order to find out a little of what we do in class. During the lesson, you will have things to do and so will Mr/Ms X. If you have any questions or queries please address them to me or you will interrupt Mr/Ms X in the course of their work. They might wish to ask you questions during the lesson. If so, answer them as fully as you can. Thank you.'

7. If the observer is to be a non -participant observer they should decide on where the observer will be located and check that the location is the best vantage point, bearing in mind the agreed focus.

8. Partners should apply the notion of 'buffer time'. This means that the teacher should, as far as possible, arrange for the lesson or activity to finish five minutes before the normally scheduled time. This will provide the observer with an opportunity to talk with pupils at the conclusion of the lesson/activity, or enable the observer to leave the room in order to add further points to the observational data whilst it is fresh in their minds. The teacher who has been observed also needs an opportunity, however limited, to make a note of their perceptions of the lesson in relation to the agreed focus. They still have responsibility for the class, but 'buffer time', where pupils can, perhaps, be set some self-sustaining work, may provide such an opportunity. Where it has been planned for the observer to talk with pupils, the teacher might make their notes then. Both parties will need to engage in further reflection and note-making, but this small sliver of 'buffer time' can have a marked effect on the quality of the feedback session.

9. After the observation the observer should make up their notes as completely as possible, separating judgements from descriptive data and giving due consideration to any inferences which may need to be cross-validated. After an interval they should look at their data again, playing the lesson through again in their minds and making a note of the key points they wish to cite in the course of the feedback session. Bear in mind that illuminative points will be shared in subsequent whole-staff discussion.

10. Keep to the agreed time and place for the feedback session.

11. Try to ensure a location which will be free of interruption.

12. The feedback session should take place within 24 hours of the observation.

Sensitive application of the skills of classroom observation is the first step in establishing a supportive and rigorous monitoring system. Observational skill needs to be accompanied by the skill of well-focused and sensitive feedback; the latter is the subject of the next chapter.

## OVERVIEW

This chapter has focused on issues relating to observing the curriculum-in-action and has presented this as a developmental process engaged in by co-professionals who are committed to supporting individual and institutional development. Ways in which prospective observer-monitors might gain insight and develop skills have been outlined and the theory of practice model proposed by Argyris and Schon has been explained and illustrated. Forms of mutual observation have been outlined as a means of extending skills still further. Twelve key points to be borne in mind when implementing policy-related observation have been identified. The source for observation is the school policy for teaching and learning and/or one of the schemes of work. Observation is a major means of ensuring that the selected part of the policy or the scheme of work is being implemented successfully.

*Chapter 6*

# The feedback process

It is a curious paradox that the majority of teachers, whilst conscious of the importance of providing feedback to the pupils in their care, have not, in the main, enjoyed the benefits of receiving systematic feedback themselves. Some teachers enjoy the advantages of an open-plan or semi open-plan environment, but for most teachers teaching is a private activity which is seldom witnessed by others. Most teachers have to rely on some form of self-evaluation of their practice. Where observation has taken place this has often been undertaken in the context of assessment or evaluation rather than development. This situation has been alleviated to a certain extent where schools have implemented appraisal with sensitive but rigorous forms of observation and feedback, but even here the frequency of observation is limited. Many teachers expressed dissatisfaction during the first wave of OFSTED inspections in terms of the paucity of feedback following classroom observation. OFSTED now requires every teacher to be given formal feedback at the end of inspection. This covers the main strengths and weaknesses observed and is followed by a written summary of the grades given. Sensitive and constructive feedback is the necessary complement to skilled observation. In this chapter, the components of the feedback process will be examined together with a framework for feedback which middle managers may find helpful in their role as observer-monitors.

## FEEDBACK AND DISCLOSURE

Feedback is one way of providing support and challenge and is intricately related to the process of disclosure. A useful model which illustrates the relationship between feedback and disclosure is that provided by the Jo-hari Window, so named after its originators, Jo Luft and Harry Ingham (see Figure 6.1). The model can be applied to any aspect of human behaviour but here it will be explained in terms of task behaviour in the work setting of the classroom.

There are parts of our behaviour which are known to ourselves and known to others. In Figure 6.1 these dimensions are represented on the horizontal side of the square. Sector 1, termed the 'public area' indicates those parts of our behaviour which are known to us and known to others. In terms of our practice as teachers this is the area in which we are likely to feel most confident and in consequence, most relaxed and 'free' as we engage in the business of promoting learning. But there may be parts of our behaviour which are known to others but are unknown to us. These constitute our 'blind area' (Sector 2). Colleagues may provide us with information on that aspect of our behaviour and we may, or we may not, act upon such information. The arrow above the word feedback in Figure 6.1 is double-headed to indicate the fact that feedback is a *two-way process*. To the extent that we respond to the information and actively seek to alter our behaviour in the light of the information, we incrementally extend our 'public area' and may in consequence become more effective in some aspect of teaching and learning. Our response is likely to be influenced by the manner in which the information is communicated, the credibility of the observer in the eyes of the teacher, and so on.

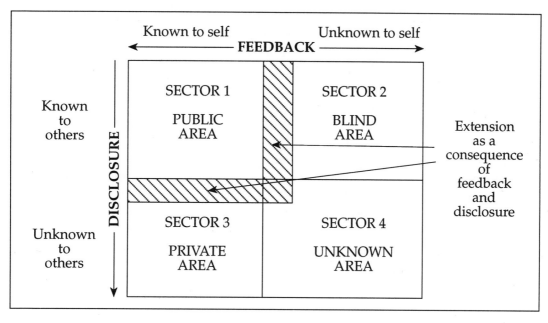

**Figure 6.1**    Jo-Hari window

The vertical dimension to Figure 6.1 relates to the process of disclosure and Sector 3 refers to the private aspects of our behaviour which are known to us but which are unknown to others. Note that the arrow of disclosure is single headed, to reflect the fact that the individual controls the decision to disclose. To the extent that the person is willing to disclose relevant information during the monitoring/feedback process the opportunity exists for them to extend their 'public area'. Willingness to disclose will be influenced by the degree of trust and interpersonal comfort generated between the parties concerned.

The final Sector, 4, is the 'unknown area' and reflects those parts of our psyche which are not available to us in the normal course of events. Such knowledge may surface as a consequence of critical incidents or traumatic events in our lives. But for our purpose here, Sector 4 represents new insights and flashes of awareness which may be suddenly stimulated during feedback and which neither the observer nor the teacher could have anticipated. During the process the opportunity exists for *each* of the partners to disclose information relevant to the focus at hand.

## ACTIVE LISTENING

Active listening has been defined as 'listening with a purpose', its purpose being to find out what is in and on someone else's mind in relation to some aspect of their life or work. It has also been defined as:

a dynamic process in which the listener attempts to gain insights into the perceptual, intellectual and emotional world of the speaker...any concerns of the listener are temporarily suspended. The whole stance is concerned to enable the talker to explore in as full and complete a way as possible their own professional ideas and concerns. (Whitaker, 1994, p.59)

Normal conversation is underpinned by tacit rules which determine the length of each person's contribution, the latter being signalled by a wide range of non-verbal cues which shape the interaction. Individuals who violate conversational norms are likely to find themselves playing a marginal role in social situations until such time as they have 'learned' the rules.

During an active listening interview these rules of normal discourse are replaced by a structure in which the interviewer speaks for about 25 per cent of the available time and the respondent for 75 per cent. This is very different from the balance within normal conversation and it is therefore helpful for each of the parties to be aware of the way the interaction is to be structured. The purpose and structure of an interview should be understood by both parties and the interviewer should indicate this at the outset. Active listening is made up of clusters of skills:

1. Establishing rapport.
   Demonstrating active attention towards the other person requires you to consider:
   • the location of the interview;
   • seating arrangements;
   • body posture and proximity between the persons concerned;
   • eye contact;
   • use of gesture/body language;
   • how dialogue will be initiated;
   • facial expression/smiling.

2. Following, supporting the respondent.
   Here, attention is being paid to how you:
   • encourage your colleague to continue their account by appropriate body language (nodding, smiling, etc.) and by the use of constructively probing questions;
   • make constructive use of silence, giving your respondent time to reflect, and conveying a sense that it is alright to pause;
   • avoid the tendency to fill silences with further questions.

3. Demonstrating understanding.
   Here you are letting your respondent know that you have understood what they have said and to do this it is useful to:
   • reflect to them what you have heard them say;
   • paraphrase what has been said;
   • periodically summarize as the interview proceeds.
   Points to avoid:
   • interrupting, which blocks the respondent's flow of thought;
   • asking leading questions, which results in your values being explored rather than those of your respondent;
   • offering advice or providing solutions, which induces dependency on the part of the respondent and reduces the likelihood that they will take responsibility for their learning.

Points to remember:
- 'park' the things which you have on your mind;
- try to avoid evaluating information as you hear it;
- act as a partner in listening mode;
- you are there to understand their world/practice not to propound yours;
- the 25–75 balance of the talk.

---

### Activity 10
### THE LISTENING INTERVIEW

Work in threes, one person being the storyteller (A), one the active listener (B) and the third the observer (C), who provides feedback to A and B at the close of the ten minute listening interview. Each person will take on each of these roles in turn. The whole session will take about 45 minutes.

Decide on three topics, allocating one to each of the colleagues. Examples might be, 'OFSTED inspection', 'Qualities of an effective teacher', or 'Standard Assessment Tasks and the National Curriculum'. The topic should be of personal relevance to the colleague concerned and, ideally, should be one on which which they are likely to have strong views, knowledge and/or experience.

Allow ten minutes preparation time in which colleagues make notes which they might use as an *aide-mémoire* when in the role of storyteller.

Carry out a ten minute listening interview. This is then followed by a feedback session which is led by the observer (C). When this has been completed, switch roles so that each person has had the opportunity to undertake each of the roles A, B and C. An observer's checklist is provided below.

---

### OBSERVER CHECKLIST

During the interview make notes on how the active listener (B):
- arranged the seating and sought to establish an appropriate environment;
- invites the respondent to present their account;
- actively listens and encourages their colleagues to keep talking;
- avoids interrupting;
- uses silences constructively and avoids filling them;
- deploys appropriate non-verbal behaviour to maintain the dynamic;
- periodically paraphrases;
- summarizes at appropriate intervals and then encourages the respondent to provide further information/ideas by their use of constructive probing questions;
- concludes the interview with a summary of the key points made by the storyteller (A).

Examples of constructively probing questions:
- 'I noticed that you mentioned...Could you say a little more about that?'
- 'What do you feel might account for...?'
- 'What might account for your feelings about this?'
- 'You have suggested one response which you might take. Do you have any other suggestions to make?'
- 'Is there any other way of looking at...?'
- 'Of the four alternatives which you outlined, which do you feel is the most likely to succeed?'
- 'What resources might help you here?'

---

## THE 30 MINUTE FEEDBACK FRAMEWORK

Figure 4.1 in Chapter 4 indicated the co-professional nature of monitoring. During observation and feedback we are concerned with task-related behaviour, not personality. Observer-monitors are agents acting on behalf of their partners and ideally the relationship between the two should be such that:
- each has credibility in the eyes of the other;

| The observer | The stages | The teacher |
|---|---|---|
| • Outlines feedback structure. Invites teacher to present their perceptions in relation to the agreed focus<br>• ACTIVELY LISTENS and does not INTERRUPT<br>• HAVING LISTENED: SUMMARIZES KEY POINTS AND ENDORSES THOSE WHICH THEIR DATA WOULD SUPPORT | **STAGE 1**<br><br>**DRAW OUT**<br><br>**AND**<br><br>**CONFIRM**<br><br>**(5 minutes)** | • Presents their perceptions and provides observational data to support same<br><br>• LISTENS TO SUMMARY AND ADDS ANY POINTS THEY HAVE OMITTED |
| • Communicates observational data not cited by the teacher in relation to the agreed focus | **STAGE 2**<br><br>**PRESENT**<br><br>**(5 minutes)** | • TEACHER ACTIVELY LISTENS TO ACCOUNT AND DOES NOT INTERRUPT |
| • Observer and teacher tease out/identify key factors influencing:<br>• strengths;<br>• points for subsequent development by the teacher | **STAGE 3**<br><br>**ANALYSE AND EXPLORE**<br><br>**(15 minutes)** | • Teacher takes shared responsibility for identifying key factors associated with extension of teacher repertoire |
| • Observer: RESPONDS TO TEACHER'S IDEAS AND APPLIES CRITERIA OF FEASIBILITY AND MANAGEABILITY. AGREES FORM(S) OF ONGOING SUPPORT | **STAGE 4**<br><br>**HAND BACK SUPPORT**<br><br>**AND**<br><br>**EMPOWER**<br><br>**(5 minutes)** | • Teacher: IDENTIFIES AND PROPOSES KEY POINTS FOR ACTION IN RELATION TO FACTORS NOTED IN STAGE 3 |

**Figure 6.2**     The 30 minute feedback framework (Based on West and Remnant, 1994.)

- both are willing to actively listen;
- both are prepared to facilitate the extension of repertoire.

The skill of active listening is central to the process of providing feedback and is a key feature of the feedback framework presented in Figure 6.2. In developing the framework, two criteria were borne in mind: the need to provide a simple but effective structure and the need for feedback to be set in a realistic time-scale. The rules of normal discourse are replaced by an agreed set of ground rules. To facilitate this the framework is comprised of four stages, each stage having a particular objective.The observer-monitor is responsible for managing the feedback session.

## Stage 1

In stage 1 the observer should remind their colleague of the four-stage structure that will be used and then invite them to present their perceptions of the agreed focus. In presenting their account the teacher may refer to their notes and where possible should cite evidence to support their perceptions. The role of the observer is to listen and encourage the flow of the account. Having actively listened to the account, the observer's job is then to summarize what they have heard and re-present this to their colleague. They are acting as a reflective mirror and should resist adding value judgements on what has been said. It is usually the case that at this point the teacher adds information which they overlooked in their initial account, or takes the opportunity to clarify, or expand upon particular points. In stage 1 the evidential base in relation to the agreed focus has, as it were, been put on the table by the teacher who was observed. Most observers feel the need to make notes of some kind during stage 1. For them not to do so may result in them attending to what they must remember and in consequence become distracted from the active listening process.

## Stage 2

During stage 2 the roles are reversed, the teacher actively listening to the analysis of their observer/monitor. In presenting their account it is useful for observers to begin by pointing out where their data cross-validates that of their colleague and then go on to present further information citing observational data to support their analysis. We now have two sets of data which fuel stage 3.

## Stage 3

Stage 3 is labelled 'analyse and explore', and here each of the partners seeks to tease out factors relevant to the agreed focus. The dialogue is likely to be hallmarked by conjecture, by conditional statements and the exploration of alternatives relating to what might follow in the light of the shared analysis. Both will bring their experience to bear, both will be interested in the alternatives, since these may illuminate issues which are important to both. *Stage 3 is not about evaluating a particular lesson, its concern is the in-depth exploration of aspects of practice relevant to the agreed focus.* It is about enhancing the match between the public map (the policy) and the private image of individual teachers (their interpretation of the policy). The focus may also be concerned with an aspect of a scheme of work and how far this is being implemented. It is also about exploring and celebrating inventive instances of the policy in action with a fellow practitioner.

**Stage 4**

During stage 4 the observer-monitor acts as critical friend to their colleague and seeks to ensure that the aspect of practice chosen by them for further development is feasible and manageable and that they are not attempting too much. Teachers must accept responsibility for their own learning in the knowledge that they have a colleague with whom they can engage in ongoing dialogue and exploration of the matter at hand. It is often the case that in the course of observation and feedback the observer-monitor gains fresh insight into a particular aspect of practice. The process is hallmarked by rigorous joint enquiry, rather than the transmission of information from one who knows to one who does not. The objective is not to prove but to improve. You don't have to be ill to get better.

## INSTITUTIONAL LEARNING

The objectives of the programmes of action are to enhance the quality of the curriculum-in-action and to promote institutional learning. In managing individual programmes a named person should undertake to collect the key findings from each monitor-observer so that the sum total of all the joint explorations can be shared and explored at staff meetings, where they form the sole item on the agenda. Such meetings should be chaired by a senior member of staff who has been closely associated with the particular programme of action. The purpose of such meetings is to enable all members of staff to be aware of:

- how far an agreed aspect of the policy for teaching and learning is understood and being implemented;
- how far schemes of work are being implemented;
- inventive and effective practice which will be of benefit to all members of the team;
- problematic aspects of teaching and learning that need further exploration and understanding;
- the aspects of practice which colleagues will continue to explore in the the course of their work;
- the range of acceptable practice in relation to a specific aspect of agreed policy;
- elements within the policy which need to be amended or added to in some way;
- where additional support is required and welcomed;
- the value of going beneath the surface features of practice;
- the value which can accrue from systematic monitoring.

The process is anchored in trust. Unlike appraisal, where data are ring-fenced by confidentiality, policy-related monitoring and feedback permit the sharing of issues relating to an agreed whole-school focus. It is not about the assessment of teachers, it is about the development of shared understanding about key aspects of the complex business of teaching and learning.

## Activity 11

## OBSERVATION AND FEEDBACK

*Objectives*
To apply and practise the skills of classroom observation and feedback.

*Task*
Work with a fellow coordinator/middle manager using the observational framework provided and the 30 minute feedback framework.

*Agreed focus*
Factors which help
Factors which hinder } the quality of pupils' learning
Blindspots (things the teacher does of which they are unaware).

Engage in non-participant observation making notes as you do so on an A4 sheet bearing the following headings:

|  Helping factors  |
| Judgements | Description |

| Hindering factors |
| Description | Judgements |

Remember to build in the 'buffer time' mentioned in Chapter 5. During buffer time fill out your notes, separating judgements from description. Be prepared to support any judgements with descriptive information. Identify any blindspots you may have noted. It is assumed that the colleague whom you have observed has also made notes of his/her perceptions of the lesson in relation to the agreed focus.

Meet at an agreed time for the feedback session (which must be within 24 hours of the observation) and apply the feedback framework bearing in mind the points made in relation to active listening and the ground rules of taking responsibility for your own learning.

At the end of the feedback session focus on the process skills you both seek to develop. Note key points which might be borne in mind during the next period of observation when roles are reversed.

---

Examples of key points noted by middle managers in the course of the first observation include:

- need to pay equal attention to teacher and pupil behaviour in noting strengths and hindrances;
- need to build in time to talk with targeted pupils:
- need to ensure that the location of the observer was the best vantage point;
- blindspots are not necessarily negative – some teachers are unaware of their strengths;
- tendency during feedback for the observer to offer solutions rather than help the teacher to explore alternatives;
- 'slippage' in terms of active listening. Framework not applied rigorously and tendency to regress to normal conversation with subsequent increase in time needed to complete the feedback;
- too many points identified for the teacher to follow up.

The skills associated with the provision of feedback can be applied in many different contexts such as parent-consultation evenings when parents are keen to receive feedback concerning their child; in the classroom when giving feedback to pupils; during staff meetings when information is requested on an agenda item; during an appraisal interview; and during planning sessions within the year-group.

The next chapter focuses on the early stages of taking up the role of coordinator/subject manager.

## OVERVIEW

This chapter has focused on the feedback process and has drawn attention to the importance of the interrelated processes of disclosure and feedback and the significance of active listening. A four-stage feedback framework has been presented as a means of ensuring consistency and making the best use of time. Systematic policy-related observation is regarded as the means of implementing an agreed policy for teaching and learning, and the importance of linking programmes of action to institutional learning has been emphasized. Staff meetings called for such a purpose should have a single item on their agenda and should be chaired by a senior member of staff. The purpose of the programme of action, monitoring and feedback is to enhance whole-school understanding on a significant aspect of teaching and learning and to promote subsequent action by members of staff. Two activities have been outlined as a means whereby coordinators/middle managers might practise and apply the process skills concerned.

# PART III

# Developing skills

*Chapter 7*

# Making a claim: preparing for the subject leader role

This chapter draws together recent initiatives relating to those middle managers now termed subject leaders and is designed to assist them when seeking a post as a subject leader or considering making an application for a programme leading to the National Qualification for Subject Leaders (NQSL).

The Teacher Training Agency (TTA) published the National Standards for Subject Leaders in May 1998. The consultation period is now complete but the government has yet to decide when programmes leading to the NQSL will commence. Holmes and Tomlinson (*TES* 17 January 1997) have noted that 'It is in the very comprehensiveness of the NQSL that its problems and challenges lie. This award is aimed simultaneously at the experienced primary teacher who coordinates two or three major subjects and at the head of faculty in a large secondary school who may have as many as twenty staff many of whom are specialists in the sub-sets of-say-science.'

The process will begin with selection procedures linked to an assessment of needs, followed by training programmes delivered by a range of providers accredited by the TTA together with a mix of IT-based distance learning materials. The TTA initiatives, starting with Initial Teacher Training (ITT), the National Literacy and Numeracy initiatives, the National Standards identified for New Teachers, Subject Leaders, Special Needs Coordinators, prospective Headteachers and the HEADLAMP programmes for serving headteachers represent the largest concerted initiative aimed at changing the culture of schools and raising the quality of teaching and learning ever mounted in England and Wales.

In their Annual Review (TTA, 1997) the TTA indicated that the standards are increasingly being used by teachers, subject leaders and headteachers to focus on professional development and to set targets, and also by LEAs and HEIs as the basis for training programmes. The core purpose and outcomes provide a useful reference point for prospective subject leaders wishing to reflect on their readiness for such a role.

## SUBJECT LEADERSHIP: CORE PURPOSE AND KEY OUTCOMES

The core purpose of subject leadership as defined by the TTA (1997) is:

> To provide professional leadership for a subject to secure high quality teaching and effective use of resources, and ensure improved standards of achievement for all pupils.

Effective subject leadership should result in:

> *Pupils* who show sustained improvement in their subject knowledge, understanding and skills in relation to prior attainment; understand the key ideas in the subject; show

improvement in their literacy, numeracy and IT skills ... and are enthusiastic about the subject and highly motivated to continue with their studies.

*Teachers* who work together well as a team; support the aims of the subject and understand how they relate to the school's aims; are involved in the formation of policies and plans and apply them consistently in the classroom; are dedicated to improving standards of teaching and learning; have an enthusiasm for the subject which reinforces the motivation of pupils; have high expectations for pupils and set realistic but challenging targets based on a good knowledge of their pupils and the progression of concepts in the subject; make good use of guidance, training and support to enhance their knowledge and understanding of the subject and to develop understanding of the subject and to develop expertise in their teaching; take account of research and inspection findings; and select appropriate teaching and learning approaches to meet subject specific learning objectives and the needs of pupils.

*Parents* who are well informed about their child's achievements in the subject and about targets for further improvement ...

*Senior managers* who understand the needs of the subject, and use information about achievements and development priorities in the subject to make well informed decisions.
(TTA, 1997, *National Standards for Subject Leaders*)

Such a key purpose and set of expectations provide food for thought for the prospective subject leader and a useful reference point for experienced subject leaders wishing to compare expectations with their existing job descriptions. Subject knowledge is an important but insufficient requirement. They have now to possess the range of sophisticated process skills outlined in Section 4 of the Standards document and most of these are explored in depth in Chapters 3 to 9. A framework for development, policy implementation, monitoring and evaluation has already been explored in depth in Chapter 3. Classroom observation, monitoring and evaluation and the provision of feedback have been explored in depth in Chapters 4, 5 and 6.

The complexity of the process skills required in the job is no more clearly indicated by HMI when they note that 'the endeavours of specialists to influence the work of other teachers rarely bring the quality of the teaching by non-specialists *up to that of the specialist*. Many middle managers feel that too much is being expected of them given to the limited resources and time at their disposal. Schools welcome the support provided by the 20-day courses designed specifically for subject leaders and other forms of resource such as those provided by the Open University in the field of Primary Science (*'Making Sense of Science' a study guide*) prepared by Patricia Murphy in which the TTA Standards provide a key reference point in the course design. Backed by ten videos, this type of programme will assist subject leaders seeking to influence the practice of their colleagues. It must be noted, however, that the use of such excellent resources will still require careful management by headteachers. Few schools can manage more than one innovation at a time.

## PREPARING TO TAKE ON THE SUBJECT LEADER ROLE: FIRST THOUGHTS

Self-audits may be undertaken at different stages in an individual's career:
  at the initial stage in an annual appraisal cycle;

when first seeking the role of subject leader;
when seeking further promotion in a different school.
The self-audit activities offered here may help at these different points.

Since leadership is a prime requisite in the job the features of transformational leadership are outlined as the chapter proceeds. An honest self-audit followed by dialogue with a critical friend or mentor is a propitious way of making a start.

---

### Activity 12
### YOUR VIEW OF YOUR ROLE

It is difficult to be an effective leader and manager if you have not thought through the requirements of the role and identified the values you hold in relation to the complex business of promoting learning and development at whole school level. This shift of perspective from that of a particular class or year-group to a whole-school perspective lies at the heart of successful subject leadership. Transcending the particular and the most familiar (your own classroom and your particular practice) to a consideration of the wider spectrum of the school is not an easy matter.

**Read the statements below and note those which best fit your current situation**
- I am a Generalist with special knowledge in child development rather than a specific subject.
- I am a Generalist with particular interest and expertise and knowledge in a particular subject but have no formal qualification in the subject concerned.
- I have specialist knowledge in one subject and would like to be a subject leader.
- I am a teacher with a specialist subject and would like to take on a Specialist role, teaching my subject as near full-time as possible.

Look through your notes and discuss them with a critical friend.
What do you think should be your next step in preparing yourself:
- For a first application as a subject leader?
- For further promotion as a subject leader?

---

Taking on a leadership role requires you to provide a sense of direction, the ability to articulate the values you hold in respect of your subject and the capacity to communicate the key features of the subject in question. To lead and manage others it is helpful if you can demonstrate to others that you can manage yourself. Two further forms of self audit follow.

---

### Activity 13
### A PERSONAL AND PROFESSIONAL SELF-AUDIT

The purpose of the audit is to heighten self-awareness in relation to a number of aspects of your role as a middle manager. Answer the questions as fully and as truthfully as possible. Make full notes on each item. Do not try to complete the audit in one go; allow yourself plenty of time for self-reflection. You may find it helpful to ask questions of colleagues on the staff. If you have a colleague in the same position as yourself, you may wish to carry out the audit individually and then share your responses with each other in the role of 'critical friend'. Ignore any questions which are inappropriate to your specific situation, or adapt the questions to suit. You will probably find that other questions occur to you as you proceed. If so, include them in your notes. The items are not presented in a particular order in order to lessen the likelihood of engendering a response-set to successive items. You will probably get more out of it if you avoid re-reading a previous question associated with the same aspect. You can then check inter-item responses for internal consistency. Remember, the objective is to construct a self-generated profile which you can then explore in terms of any gaps, ambiguities, or personal dilemmas.

---

## Teaching and learning

- What would you identify as the key educational principles which underpin your practice?
- What examples from your own practice would you cite to illustrate those principles in action?
- What do think should characterize pupil learning in the curriculum or Key Stage area which you coordinate?
- How familiar are you with documentation relating to the National Curriculum?
- What do you consider to be the contribution of your particular curriculum area to the curriculum as a whole?
- Can you give examples of contemporary teaching and learning resources associated with your curriculum area?
- What form(s) should pupil assessment, recording and reporting take in your curriculum area?
- In what ways have you recently extended your understanding of the curriculum area or Key Stage for which you are accountable?
- Could you describe three different examples of high quality teaching and learning in your curriculum area or Key Stage?
- What changes would you like to introduce to this area/aspect of the school's work?

## Professional knowledge and experience

- What do you understand by the terms 'leadership' and 'management'?
- How would you define the term 'monitoring'?
- How do you/would you monitor quality in the area/aspect for which you have responsibility?
- What would you identify as the key skills and competences required in the post you are seeking or the post you currently hold?
- How would you respond to a situation in which some members of staff appeared reluctant to engage in an initiative that you were leading?
- Can you provide an illustrative example of an initiative which you have led in your current school in the past year?
- What whole-school initiatives have you been associated with in the past 12 months?
- What would you identify as the key issues in the current debate concerning your curriculum area or the aspect of the school associated with your post?
- How do you/would you engage in the process of identifying INSET needs relating to your area of responsibility?
- In what ways do you think it appropriate to offer support to staff?
- How do you/would you involve governors in your work in the school?
- Which educational journals/papers do you a) read regularly, b) dip into occasionally?
- What do you consider to be the characteristics of an effective team?
- How would you characterize your leadership style?
- How would you rate your level of interpersonal skill?
- What ideas do you have on improving levels of staff motivation?

# LEADERSHIP AND VISION

In the contemporary literature on leadership, emphasis is increasingly placed on the value of what is termed 'transformational leadership' in which 'leaders and followers are united in pursuit of higher level goals common to both. Both want to shape the school in a new direction' (Sergiovanni, 1990, p.24). Transformational leadership seeks to move the culture of the school towards more extended forms of collaboration and it is not surprising that this form of leadership has been identified as a significant factor in school improvement. The concepts of empowerment and vision building are also strongly associated with transformational leadership. An organizational vision has been defined by Bennis and Nanus (1985) as, 'A mental image of a possible and desirable future state of the organisation...a view of a realistic, credible, attractive future for the organisation, a condition that is better in some important ways than what now exists'. Barth (1988) has defined schools as 'four walls surrounding the future' and added, in relation to vision building:

I believe that the character and quality of schools will dramatically improve when those who work in schools – teachers, students and principals – come in touch with their own visions about the way they would like their schools to be and take deliberate steps to move in those directions.

To construct an image of the future implies working through a critique of the present. One way of engaging in such a critique is to focus upon what Murgatroyd (1989) has called 'moments of truth' i.e:

The critical moments at which the culture and values of the school are expressed through the action of a teacher, or the head, or the secretary, or some other agent of the school…At these moments the quality of the school as an experience is immediately available to the participant: it is a moment at which the truth about the nature of school as an experience is real for the participant.

Reflecting on the incidence and nature of such moments in the school as a whole may stimulate insights into what might be done differently.

There are contrasting views on the ways in which a vision statement should be formulated. Peters and Austin (1985) suggest that a vision,

must always, we observe, start with a single individual. We are wary, to say the least, of 'committee visions'. That does not mean that a major team effort of re-writing and buy ins should not ensue. It usually should. But the raw material of the effective vision is invariably the result of one man's or woman's souls searching.

Fullan and Hargreaves (1992, p.123) see vision building as part of a collaborative culture: 'Collaboration should mean creating the vision together, not complying with the head's own…. The articulation of different voices may create initial conflict, but this should be confronted and worked through. It is part of the collaborative mix'. Where coordinators have the opportunity to participate in vision building, each member of the team has the opportunity to present their 'educational platform', the latter being comprised of their assumptions and beliefs on such issues as the way children learn, how learning is to be celebrated in the school, how quality is to be monitored and how support is to be provided for pupils and staff. Visions have to be lived out by all the individuals within an organization, including the formal leader for whom they carry the same implications as everyone else on the team. In Block's (1987) words, 'The hardest thing for any of us is to live by the rules that we create…When we create a vision for our unit, we create a set of requirements and demands on ourselves'.

A vision statement reflects values but it is not couched in broad philosophical terms. Its essential feature is that it conveys sharp images of what the school wishes to work towards. It has also been suggested that a vision statement should have a certain outrageousness which helps drives it forward. An illustration of a vision statement is given below. In this example the school expresses its vision in terms of the characteristics it wishes to establish within the team. Get this in place, the logic runs, and everything else will follow for the key client – the pupils. A different school might couch their statement in terms of the curriculum and how learning is to be characterized.

…we intend to establish a school which has the characteristics of an intellectual community in which dialogue on the complexities of practice is to be welcomed and encouraged. We do not accept an image of our school as a place where pupils learn and teachers teach. We seek to build a community of professionals committed to the pursuit of quality in which staff willingly submit their practice to constructive observation, analysis and feedback. Constructive monitoring is regarded as the means of implementing whole-school policy.

Staff will be expected to take responsibility for their own learning with the support of colleagues who share the same endeavour. All staff are asked to recognize that if they are unwilling to be part of a solution they remain part of everyone else's problem.

Our core aim is the constant improvement of the quality of learning experiences offered to pupils. The citing of evidence, reference to relevant literature and engagement in the processes of critical reflection are seen as the hallmark of a team devoted to the pursuit of quality.

This vision statement should be read in conjunction with the school's policy for teaching and learning.

---

### Activity 14
### VISION BUILDING

1. As a way of starting your thinking about the process of building a vision, you are asked to imagine that it is 2000 and your school has just received formal acknowledgement from OFSTED that it is a school of outstanding merit. Complete the citation which begins:

_____school is a school of outstanding merit in which the everyday experiences of pupils fit well with its published vision statement. There was strong evidence to support...

(Try to form sharp images of what might have been witnessed at the school; for example, what characterized teaching and learning, staff relationships, home-school relations, etc.)

2. Compare what you have written with your current perceptions of your school. What aspects do you think the school might work on?

3. Complete the following statements:

• I would like the school to become the kind of place where...

• As a teacher I would like my colleagues to...

• If I left this school the image I would take away is...

• When I reflect on the ways in which our pupils engage in learning I think we should...

• In terms of staff collaboration I would like to see...

4. In the light of the preceding activities:

   a) what key points would you wish to contribute to the vision building process?

   b) what vision do you have of the curriculum area/aspect of the school for which you are responsible?

---

## TAKING UP A SUBJECT-MANAGER ROLE IN A DIFFERENT SCHOOL

On taking up a post in a different school it is useful to reflect on aspects of the school before you become socialized into the norms of your new work setting. The purpose of the following activity is to enable you to become aware of the culture of the school in which you are working and consider what strategies are most likely to be successful in your new role.

In the light of your responses how would you typify the culture of your school in terms of the three levels of collaboration outlined in Chapter 2? Each level is capable of change, given appropriate leadership and a common will. Hopkins *et al.* (1994), drawing on the work of Rosenholtz (1989) suggest a continuum of school types in which

---

## Activity 15
## TAKING ON THE ROLE OF SUBJECT LEADER

The following questions will help you to become aware of the characteristics of the culture of your new school. Some of the questions are relatively straightforward, but it may only be possible to answer some of them after you have talked with colleagues. Reflect on 'the way things are done around here'; notice what happens in meetings and how staff in a similar role to you go about their job as a subject leader.

### Starting the job: perceptions, expectations and feelings

- How are you feeling about your new job?
- What are the staff's perceptions of your predecessor?
- What will be your first initiative? On what grounds?
- In what ways do you think that you are a) similar to and b) different from your predecessor?
- What do you think staff expect from you in your role as subject leader?
- What strengths do you feel you have that others may find useful?
- Do you have any characteristics that some members of staff might find off-putting?
- Are you a punctual person? Do you arrive at meetings on time?
- If you had a problem in your role as a subject leader, which member of staff do you think you would turn to for help? Why?
- Which members of staff constitute your major role-set?
- What information do you have on the background, knowledge and experience of your fellow subject leaders?
- What expectations do you think the staff have of you in your role as a subject leader?
- What are your expectations of other subject leaders?

### About your role

- Do you have a job description?
- Does your job description identify your key tasks and responsibilities and to whom you are accountable?
- Do others know what is in your job description and do you know what is in theirs?
- What are your current key goals? Who identified them?
- How do you intend to achieve these goals? Do you have an action plan? Has anyone seen your action plan and given you feedback?
- How do you intend to demonstrate good practice in your classroom?
- Have you been given 'authority to act' by the headteacher and has this been communicated to all members of staff?
- Are you familiar with the resources available to you in terms of your role as a subject leader?

---

four expressions of school culture can be identified. These are termed 'stuck' schools ('learning impoverished' schools in Rosenholtz's terms), 'wandering' schools (which have experienced and are experiencing too much innovation); 'promenading' schools (often traditional schools with a stable staff that have enjoyed success in more stable times but are currently reluctant to change) and 'moving' schools (the second of Rosenholtz's original typology and which are characterized by adaptiveness, balance between maintenance and development, and staff who are committed to the notion that learning about teaching and learning is an ongoing process. In 'moving' schools, giving and receiving help are not associated with incompetence and they have the features of extended forms of collaboration. Every school has the latent potential to move across such a continuum and coordinators who have the acuity to recognize indicators for change have a valuable role to play in their school's development. Even within schools of the first three types there may well be subgroups of staff who seek to change the dominant culture of the school.

This chapter has presented activities relevant to those middle managers termed subject leaders who are taking up the role for the first time or who are undertaking the role in a new school. Chapter 8 focuses on additional skills required in the job.

# OVERVIEW

Undertaking a self-audit prior to taking on the role of subject manager should have the benefit of clarifying personal values and the rationale which informs your work. To have reviewed personal values and beliefs pertinent to what is needed should make for more effective management and leadership than might otherwise be the case. Much will depend on the capacity to engage in meaningful self-analysis and in so doing identify where there is a need to extend existing knowledge, develop new skills, or acquire experiences relevant to the post. Where a school has a well-planned induction scheme for new staff and for staff new in role, this will provide opportunities for well-focused dialogue.

A school culture characterized by transformational leadership, shared vision and a commitment to the empowerment of others provides the optimum work setting for a newly appointed subject manager. Self-auditing prior to or following appointment will enable managers to play a more informed role in the vision building process. In the situation where the school is not at the extended part of the cultural continuum, it is still possible for individuals to work within the dominant culture in productive ways.

*Chapter 8*

# Developing middle management skills

This chapter seeks to assist subject managers/Key Stage coordinators who wish to extend the skills required of them in their job. The areas covered are:
- leading the team
- delegation
- managing change
- leading an evaluation
- finance and resource management
- self-management and
- management of time.

## LEADING THE TEAM

In earlier chapters of this book it has been proposed that the complex goals of primary schools will be best achieved by means of a mixed economy of designated individual roles associated with maintenance tasks and the use of project or task teams to achieve developmental goals. Middle managers will therefore be involved for some of their time as *leaders* of a task-oriented group. A team is effective when it achieves the goals which have been set through tasks which have been identified and agreed between members. A team is efficient to the extent that it uses resources economically and produces results which are practical, appropriate and acceptable to team members and those affected by the outcomes. Put briefly, effectiveness is about 'doing the right thing' and efficiency is about 'doing things right'.

Leadership has been defined as 'the process of influencing the activities of an organized group towards goal achievement' (Rauch and Belling, 1984). Figure 8.1 shows two dimensions to leadership behaviour. In leading a group the leader has to demonstrate awareness of two basic concerns: concern for people and concern for task.

Situation 'A' in Figure 8.1 reflects high concern for people at the expense of concern for task and is likely to result in positive social rapport but relatively poor task achievement. Verbal stroking and socializing may get you liked but it might not bring results.

'B' represents an abdication of leadership by the leader who shows low concern for task (it may have been an imposed task which was never owned) and low concern

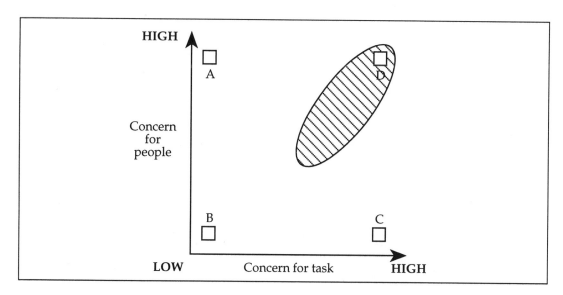

**Figure 8.1**    Dimensions to leadership behaviour

for people. This may be due to indifference on the part of the leader or due to an assumption on the part of the leader that the team can achieve the task without much help from them. It indicates an abdication of the key concerns of leadership.

Situation 'C' represents a rather driven situation in which task requirements take precedence over concern for people. The task(s) may be achieved but the psychological needs of group members may not have been met. Such a team may be reluctant to engage in future groupwork with the leader concerned.

Situation 'D' represents an effective balance between concern for team members and a proper concern for the achievement of the agreed task(s). It represents an ideal position which effective leaders seek to bring about. Few leaders achieve this, most oscillating within the shaded area indicated in Figure 8.1.

The manner in which leadership is articulated by leaders has been referred to as their 'leadership style', effective leaders being those who are able to apply a style of leadership which matches the task-related needs of the individual or group with whom they are working. In choosing the style, a balance has to be maintained between those behaviours directed at getting the task accomplished (task-related behaviour by the leader) and those behaviours which are directed towards the personal needs of the individual or group (relationship behaviour), either of which might be high or low. The leader first makes an estimation of the ability of the person or group concerned to undertake the task. Ability is defined in terms of knowledge or previous experience of the task requirements together with an estimation of their degree of confidence and willingness to undertake the task. In the light of this, the situational leader decides on the appropriate mixture of task/person-related behaviour which they should adopt in the given situation. Situational leadership is a far cry from approaches to leadership defined in terms of personality types or traits and is fully developed in Hersey and Blanchard (1988). Models of situational leadership are useful illuminative frameworks worthy of exploration by middle managers, but it is even more important for them to be aware of the predispositions which shape their leadership behaviour, particularly when they exercise leadership or find themselves working in an area in which values are contested. The following activity may sensitize you to those predispositions which may be attributable to you at this time.

## Characteristics of an effective team

Such a team:

- shares an understanding of the goals it seeks to achieve;
- converts the goals into a set of agreed tasks;
- identifies what will count as success criteria in meeting the goal;
- actively listens to the suggestions and ideas of others;
- is aware of the parameters of the authority granted to the team;
- agrees a set of procedures appropriate to the achievement of the task(s);
- assigns appropriate functional roles in relation to the task;
- reviews progress and promotes learning within the group;
- is able to deal with disagreements in a constructive way;
- meets its goals in the allotted time-scale;
- evaluates its strengths and weaknesses in the light of results achieved.

Adair (1986), writing on effective leadership, identifies three dimensions to the process:

- achieving the task;
- building and maintaining the team;
- developing the individual within the team.

The team leader needs to pay attention to each of these dimensions as the team engages in its work, and in developing the team should seek to foster the capacity within the team to take care of its members. Figure 8.2 presents a matrix of issues which middle managers may find helpful as they engage in leading a task group.

It is often difficult for a team leader, who is heavily engaged with a group, to be aware of the characteristics of the group at work. It is very easy for this to be overlooked, and in consequence the group has no really effective way of examining its effectiveness. This being so it is useful to invite a member of the group to take on the role of 'process observer', such a role being undertaken by different members of the group at different stages in the group's work. If you have not led a task group it

| KEY FUNCTIONS/ ACTIONS | TASK | TEAM | INDIVIDUAL |
|---|---|---|---|
| DEFINE GOALS | Clarify goals<br>Establish time-scale<br>Gather information<br>Identify requisite resources<br>Establish parameters of authority | Select/assemble team<br>Explain goal and rationale<br>Generate commitment<br>Encourage questions | Check that individuals understand goals<br>Respond to questions and expressions of concern<br>Involve each person |
| PLAN AND DECIDE | Identify options<br>Investigate how to make best use of skills of members<br>Plan timing of events<br>Check resource needs<br>Identify success criteria<br>Generate ownership of plan | Consult with team<br>Brainstorm ideas<br>List suggestions<br>Agree priorities<br>Agree success criteria | Listen to suggestions<br>Identify/assess abilities relevant to the task<br>Coach relevant skills as required |
| ORGANIZE AND BRIEF | Establish procedures<br>Draw up brief and action plan<br>Check individual understanding of roles and tasks<br>Listen to and respond to feedback | Set up appropriate structures and agree on sub-tasks<br>Communicate agreed plan<br>Take questions and queries<br>Delegate tasks<br>Finalize plan | Check understanding of individual roles<br>Reward commitment and enthusiasm<br>Reward good ideas<br>Invite feedback |
| CONTROL, SUPPORT AND MONITOR | Report progress to key stakeholders at agreed intervals<br>Amend action plan as necessary<br>Set examples<br>Maintain commitment to goals | Coordinate work of sub-groups<br>Check resources are in use<br>Provide feedback on tasks<br>Deal with disagreements/conflict<br>Celebrate sub-goal achievement<br>Resolve emergent problems | Provide support to individuals<br>Encourage disclosure of problems<br>Recognize individual achievements<br>Reassure where necessary<br>Check agreed deadlines are on course |
| EVALUATE/ REVIEW | Evaluate goal achievement by applying agreed success criteria<br>Report on team performance<br>Consider future action<br>Note potential improvements<br>Recognize and celebrate achievement | Give feedback on achievement<br>Invite team to review their effectiveness<br>Identify learning/insights gained | Provide individual feedback on goal achievement<br>Recognize individual development<br>Recognize contributions made to the team<br>Gather individual perceptions of teams effectiveness |

**Figure 8.2**  Leading the team: key functions

is useful to undertake the role of process observer in relation to a working group of which you are a member. The experience is invaluable in raising insights into aspects of team effectiveness.

---

## Activity 17

## OBSERVING A TEAM AT WORK

Select a team activity to observe as a non-participant observer. You may have an opportunity to take on such a role during a staff INSET day, which often requires groupwork to be undertaken under the direction of a leader. Alternatively, design a team activity for your staff which you might undertake with a year-group, or a department of the school. Ask a fellow middle manager to act as a process observer to the group and give feedback on the working of the group. Alternatively, you may like to use the 'Canes and String' task described below.

### Canes and string

The task requires between eight and 12 members in the team, who engage in the task without any further instruction other than those supplied below. If the task can be undertaken concurrently by two teams of staff, each occupying adjacent rooms, this adds to the occasion. Each group should have its own non-participant observer. An *aide-mémoire* for them to use is given below.

Materials required by each group: 36 five-foot bamboo canes, a six-inch ball of string or binder twine and one pair of scissors. These materials are placed in the centre of the room together with an A4 sheet of paper bearing the following instruction:

'The task of the group is to make a free-standing structure containing the largest volume using only the materials supplied'.

### Process observer's *aide-mémoire*

THINGS TO LOOK FOR:

- Participation: Did all the members have opportunities to participate? Were some excluded? Was any attempt made by anyone to involve marginal members in the task? Did a few people dominate?

- Leadership: Did a leader, as such, emerge? Did the group designate a leader? Did anyone make a bid to lead the group? Was the leadership shared? Did the group adopt a structure of any kind?

- Roles: Who initiated ideas? Were they supported and by whom? Did anyone block? Who helped to push the adoption of particular ideas?

- Decision making: Did the group engage in planning of any kind? Did the group start taking action without much discussion or agreement? Who helped to influence the decisions?

- Communication: What characterized the communication within the group? Did members listen to the opinions of others? Did anyone check the understanding of group members?

- Sensitivity: Did members demonstrate concern for each other? Did any members of the team try to bring in members who were at the margins of the group? What feelings did the group express at different points in the activity?

When giving feedback to the group do not refer to anyone by name. Refer to individuals in such terms as: one person, a minority, some members, the leader, the group.

Present a short summary of your observations to the group after the group has completed the task.

Relate any illuminative comments expressed by members as the group proceeded in its work (e.g. 'What are we supposed to be doing?', 'Let's stop the talking and start doing something', ' I told you it wouldn't work but you wouldn't listen', or 'You lash whilst I whip'.

---

## Activity 18
## TEAM REVIEW

When you engage as a task group leader it may be helpful to distribute copies of the following review sheet and ask each member of the group to complete their perception of the working of the team. The key characteristics can then be fed back to the team and a joint decision can be made about what might be done in the light of the analysis.

**Team review sheet**

1. Objectives: How clear were we about the purpose and objectives of the task?
   Unclear•..............•.....................•................•..............Clear

2. Planning: Did the team engage in exploring alternatives and reach an agreed plan?
   Not very effectively•..............•.................•...................•............Very effectively

3. Organization: Was our organization suitable for the task?
   Unsuitable •..............•.................•.................•..............Very suitable

4. Resources: Did we make effective use of the agreed resources?
   Ineffective•..............•.................•.................•..............Very effective

5. Participation: Did every member of the team play a full part?
   Low involvement•..............•.................•...................•.......... High involvement

6. Leadership: How effective was the style of leadership adopted?
   Rarely effective•..............•............•.................•...........Wholly effective

7. Monitoring: Was progress towards the achievement of the task well monitored?
   No monitoring evident •.......... •............. •............. •........... consistent monitoring

8. Time: Was the available time used well?
   Badly•.............•.................•............•..............Very well

9. Motivation: How do you feel about the outcomes of the team's work?
   Dissatisfied•.................•.....................•..............•..............Very pleased

10 Task: Did the team achieve the task?
   No...............Yes................

11. Strengths: What would you say were the strengths of the team?
.................................................................................................................................................
.................................................................................................................................................
.................................................................................................................................................

12. What aspects of its work does the team need to work on?
.................................................................................................................................................
.................................................................................................................................................
.................................................................................................................................................

Subject leaders comprise one of the most important resources a school possesses. What they individually and collectively achieve will affect the quality of teaching and learning and help the school to take on the characteristics of the 'moving school'. The TTA stresses the importance of working as a team and acting as an appropriate role model for pupils and other staff. It is healthy for subject managers to reflect on their effectiveness, how they relate to each other and the contribution they make to the school. The next activity is designed to help you in that task.

# DELEGATION

The TTA points out the need for subject leaders 'to devolve responsibilities and delegate tasks as appropriate' (Part 4 paragraph vii). As has been argued in Chapter 2, tasks may be delegated to an individual or to a team. In either case it is helpful to be aware of what constitutes effective delegation. The TTA document indicates the kinds of task to be delegated to subject leaders. For example:

the evaluation of teaching and learning in the subject;

the identification, selection and deployment of resources;

the dissemination of good practice;

the communication to parents and governors on the key features of the subject and its relationship to the curriculum as a whole;

leading whole-school training days; formulating schemes of work.

In small schools it will be necessary to delegate such tasks to task groups whilst in large schools middle managers and subject leaders may well delegate certain tasks to others. A survey on a recent management programme revealed that the following tasks had been delegated by middle managers: the induction of newly appointed classroom assistants; collating performance data; stocktaking of resources; reviewing the quality of book stocks and computer software; drawing up rotas; evaluating the use of resources in mathematics in particular year-groups; drawing up a scheme of work in art; producing a school performance for parents; planning a school journey; redesigning a sports day and coordinating an inter-school project on the internet.

### What do we mean by delegation?

Management has been defined as 'the achievement of tasks with and through others' and Whitaker (1993) has proposed that this being so 'enables a manager to share tasks and activities with others, and helps in the development of skills and abilities in those to whom the work is delegated, enabling them to take on progressively more complex and challenging work'. Delegation is not simply giving someone else a job to do or, even worse, regarding it as the delegation of *responsibility* to another. You cannot delegate *responsibility* since this is an attribute acquired in the execution of the task. It is, however, essential that all members of staff understand who has been given *authority* to act. For staff not to know this creates uncertainty and makes the delegatee's task more difficult than it needs to be. Delegation may be defined as:

> The transfer of a task, or set of tasks to another together with the resources required and the transfer of the appropriate authority to act.

## STAGES IN THE DELEGATION PROCESS

**Stage 1. What should be borne in mind when delegating?**

1. What is the task that is to be delegated?
   What is the objective or target?
2. What criteria will be used in assessing whether the task has been successfully achieved?
3. What are the levels of skill and competence required for successful completion of the task?
4. To what degree does the delegatee possess the skills and competences?
5. Has the person concerned had any previous experience of the task in question?
6. If there is no one in the team with the necessary skills decide what level of training will be required and engage in the training process.
7. Decide on the timespan for the completion of the task together with agreed points for feedback and review of progress.
8. Identify the resources necessary for the completion of the task.

In a period of rapid change there will be an increasing number of occasions when the task is entirely new and also calls for new skills and competences. It is useful to make a distinction here between a puzzle and a problem. A puzzle is a situation to which a solution already exists in the world and the economical way forward is to search for the solution (which may be held by a local school). A problem is a situation in which there is no known solution and here the only way to proceed is to adopt a problem-solving approach. This provides an excellent learning opportunity which might be taken on by a small task group under the leadership of a skilled facilitator who breaks the task into sub-stages and follows these with regular feedback sessions. Leadership of the group may change as the task proceeds and the next sub-task is identified. This strategy, termed planned developmental opportunities (PDOs) has proved to be a useful way forward. (See West, 1991.)

**Stage 2. Managing the process**

It is important for the manager to keep in touch with the delegatee and provide feedback on progress to date. In short, delegation is not abdication. The delegatee needs to be given a sense that they 'own the task' and should be given the space to decide on how they will proceed. It is likely that the plan will be altered as the task proceeds. Agreed feedback points provide opportunities to acknowledge particularly inventive strategies adopted by the delegatee. As the task proceeds monitor the outcomes. Encourage but don't interfere.

**Stage 3. Evaluating outcomes of the delegated task**

Apply the agreed criteria for success and identify what has been learned. Bear in mind that some of the best opportunities for learning are derived out of failure. At the final debriefing it is almost more important to ask 'What have we learned?' than 'Did we succeed?' Remember to inform all staff of the outcomes and thank them for their cooperation. Identify and agree any follow-up tasks that need to be done and who is to undertake them.

# MANAGING CHANGE

Chapter 3 of this book presented a framework for whole-school development in which middle managers, working in task groups, would undertake the role of monitoring as a key strategy in implementing a policy for teaching and learning. Another word for change is learning, and the key to success is to ensure, as far as possible, that learning is equal to, or greater than, the requirements of change. One of the most important factors in the change process is the experience that individuals have of previous changes. If, as a subject manager, you are leading a change initiative it is useful to first think of an innovation which you were involved in and which was relatively successful.

---

### Activity 20
### REFLECTING ON CHANGE

Think of a specific change which has taken place in your school in the course of the last two years. This is likely to have been associated with the implementation of the National Curriculum or it may have been a change such as the adoption of a new reading scheme, the introduction of focused teaching, or a change in the way parents are involved in the work of the school. Make notes starting from when the idea was first mooted, the broad stages which were enacted in adopting the change and the time-scale involved. If you find it difficult to remember the stages in the process, your headteacher or assistant head may be able to help you. Having done so, try to consider the innovation in more detail, and in particular try to identify the factors which contributed to its introduction. You may find it useful to draw on the following questions:

1. How, or with whom, did the idea for change originate?
2. Who were the main supporters/proposers of the change?
3. Who gave the change their support initially?
4. Would you define the change as a radical change, with marked implications for staff, or one which was in keeping with existing norms and practices?
5. How did/does the change affect you?
6. Do you think that the change was needed in the school?
7. What efforts were made to prepare/equip staff for the change?
8. What barriers to the change existed?
9. How were these barriers tackled?
10. How long did it take to implement the changes?
11. Do you think that the innovation will continue in its present form?
12. Look through your responses and list the factors that contributed to the successful adoption of the change.
13. List the staff who played a significant role at particular points in the change process.
14. What implications do you draw which might assist you when you are leading a change initiative within your school?

---

## Planning for change

Figure 8.3 indicates the broad stages which constitute the change cycle.

In planning change the first steps are those of thinking through the rationale for change:

- identifying unmet needs;
- identifying the need for change;
- deciding on what form the change might take;
- developing a clear image of what the change will look like when it has been implemented;
- identifying what will be the benefits of the change and the main beneficiaries;
- gathering information on the proposed change;
- agreeing on the need for change;
- establishing the rationale which underpins the proposed change;
- identifying the resources which will be required to bring about the planned change;
- identifying individuals who are likely to resist change and those who are ready to support it – try to minimize the resistance and maximize the forces for change;
- identifying membership of the group which will manage the change process and identifying key roles;
- identifying what will count as evidence of successful implementation.

All these will require consultations with staff and, once agreed, an initial action plan can be constructed. It is tempting to say that all of the above constitute the easy bit. The challenge lies in the process of implementation.

Fullan (1991) drew attention to the need to generate shared meanings in relation to the *what* of change and the *how* of change. He pointed out that 'It is possible to be

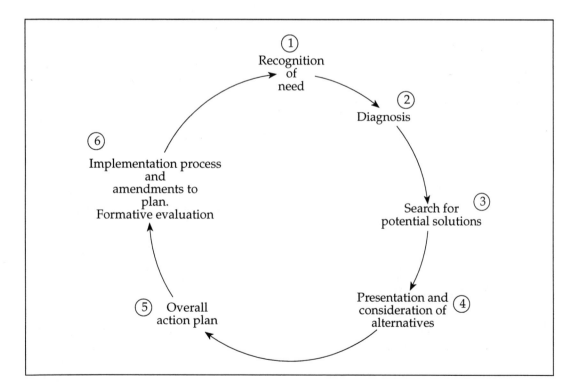

**Figure 8.3**     Stages in the change process

crystal clear about what one wants and be totally inept at achieving it. Or to be skilled at managing change but empty headed about what changes are most needed' (p.5). One of the characteristics of Rosenholtz's 'moving' schools referred to in Chapter 7 was that they had established shared meanings.

Constructive monitoring to assist policy implementation outlined in this book is based on the assumption that individuals make different interpretations of an agreed change, and that monitoring through task teams is a better means of bringing about shared meanings than individual subject-managers working on their own.

The role played by perception in shaping behaviour needs to be constantly borne in mind. In seeking to implement change, members of the task group may find the following principles based on Fullan, 1991, helpful:

- Implementing change is a process, not an event. It requires us to pay attention to many factors over a substantial period of time.
- As the change is taken up by members of staff, they will be likely to modify it in some way. Assume that this will happen; expect it. Do not think staff are giving you a hard time. It may be due to a lack of knowledge or understanding on their part, or it may be due to their desire to adapt the change in a way that does not require them to change their practice or beliefs. Be prepared to run workshops which will help staff to widen their understanding of what is involved.
- Individuals are unlikely to change their beliefs on the basis of rationality and knowledge alone. Knowledge and understanding of what is involved are necessary, but successful experimentation is much more likely to lead to a change in attitude.
- Changing practice takes time. Be prepared to demonstrate what is required and move from the simple to the complex.
- Start where people are rather than from where you would like them to be.
- Let people take risks as securely as possible.
- Have an implementation plan, but be prepared to change it in the light of events.
- Maintain the pressure for change. It is unlikely that subject-managers will be able to sustain an innovation unless it has the active support of the headteacher and senior staff.
- Managing the implementation of change is itself a learning process. Such learning will be enhanced where change is managed by a task group of middle managers rather than by one person acting in isolation.
- Keep to the agreed time-scale.
- Ensure that the implementation group engages in formative evaluation as change effort proceeds.
- Agree on when an evaluation of the change will take place and who will be involved.

## LEADING AN EVALUATION AND PREPARING AN EVALUATION REPORT

### Leading an evaluation

It may be that you have not engaged in the processes of review, monitoring or evaluation (RM&E). If this is the case you may find it useful at this stage to complete Activity 21 below.

**Activity 21**

Answer the following questions as fully as you can at this point in your career as a subject leader.
1. In which areas of the curriculum have you engaged in review, monitoring or evaluation in the course of the last year?
2. What was *your* role in these processes? (What did you do and how?)
3. Which aspects did you find particularly satisfying?
4. Were there any aspects which you found difficult or problematic?
5. Did you produce a written report on your findings?
   Was the report disseminated?
6. How would you define yourself in terms of RM&E?
   • as knowledgeable?
   • as experienced?
   • as a beginner in these processes?
7. Which aspects of RM&E would you find it helpful to explore?
8. Who might assist you in acquiring such skills?

Middle managers will be involved at various times in the interrelated processes of review, monitoring and evaluation. Earlier chapters of this book dealt in some detail with monitoring the quality of the curriculum-in-action and monitoring was seen as the key to implementing an agreed policy for teaching and learning or part of a scheme of work. It was suggested that this was best undertaken by a task group of subject managers. Evaluation is a more complex process and, since it is time-consuming, it is best undertaken periodically.

Evaluation answers the question, 'What is the merit or worth of what we do?' and has been defined as 'the systematic collection and interpretation of evidence leading, as part of the process, to a judgement of value with a view to action' (Beeby, 1987). There are seven stages to the evaluation process:
  • the planning stage;
  • initiating the process;
  • systematic collection of information;
  • processing the information (which will involve analysis and interpretation);
  • reporting the findings;
  • implementing the findings and recommendations;
  • monitoring the changes.

*1. The planning stage*

It is important for the middle manager to be able to answer the following questions before starting the evaluation:
  • *Who* wants the evaluation carried out and what is seen as its main purpose? (Is it an accountability exercise, an opportunity to diagnose a problem of some kind, is it to enable a decision to be taken, is it to examine the merit or worth of the object of the evaluation? Or is it some combination of purposes?)
  • *What* is to be the subject of the evaluation?
  • *When* is the evaluation to take place?
Having agreed that the proposed evaluation is useful, and feasible in the suggested time-scale, thought can then be given to such questions as:
  • Which members of staff will be members of the evaluation team?
  • What will be their roles? (e.g., assuming the middle manager will coordinate and lead the evaluation, who else might be involved as information gatherers?)

- What kinds of information will be collected, from whom and how?
- Who will present the evaluation report and in what form?

*2. The initiation stage*

All staff should be informed of the intended evaluation, its purpose and time-scale. Staff should then be invited to identify issues which they feel would be relevant to the evaluation. These are best gathered through discussions with individual members of staff or with key stakeholders if it is not possible to talk with everyone. Having done so, construct an 'issues agenda' of points which are of concern to members of staff. Explain to staff how information might be collected (e.g., by interviews; observations of various kinds; the analysis of documentary evidence; or by the use of a questionnaire) and check that the methods for data collection are acceptable to the people concerned. Gain agreement on what will constitute criteria for judgements in the course of the evaluation. If, for example, you were evaluating the quality of cooperative groupwork it would be useful to establish a working definition of what is meant by 'cooperative groupwork', and what would constitute illustrative examples of high quality using such an approach. This might lead to identifying characteristics that we might witness in the course of observation, the range and standards of pupils' work that might result and the value that pupils attributed to groupwork. It is essential that such criteria are identified and agreed at the initiation stage. If information is to be collected from stakeholders other than staff (parents for example) then the methods of collection need to be agreed.

*3. The collection of data*

This involves the collection of information under the agreed terms and includes the collection of responses from key respondents. The agreed time schedule should be kept to. It is sometimes the case that during this stage fresh insights are stimulated and new questions are identified. Where this is the case the information should be shared with all staff and incorporated in this phase of the evaluation.

*4. Processing the information*

Much will depend on the type(s) of information which has been collected but it is useful to consider how the information might a) be analysed, and b) subsequently presented in a way which illuminates the characteristics which have been found. You might for example:
- progressively focus on a series of key issues and illustrate these by reference to the data collected;
- present the data in terms of a series of contrasting types;
- identify common patterns and hidden norms;
- sort out facts, values, opinions and arguments expressed by respondents;
- use diagrams, tables and graphs where appropriate;
- profile the data in terms of a continuum of different types.

*5. Reporting the findings*

The following structure is helpful in preparing an evaluation report:

## A. Introduction

- the subject of the evaluation;
- the key purposes of the evaluation;
- the range and scale of the evaluation, its time span and any conscious limitations which should be borne in mind by the reader;
- the intended audience for the report.

## B. The focus of the evaluation

- the key issues/questions which were addressed in the course of the evaluation;
- the information that it was necessary to collect given the above key issues.

## C. The methods used

- how the information was collected, from whom, and by what means;
- the criteria used in the course of the evaluation.

## D. Main findings

- present the main findings in order of importance;
- cite the key points of argument or key sets of information which support each key point.

## E. Conclusions and recommendations

The inclusion of the final section depends on whether the evaluation team were expected to make recommendations. It is sometimes the case that an evaluation report simply presents the findings, any recommendations being seen as the province of a decision-making group which requested the evaluation. Where recommendations are left to the evaluation team it is important for them to check the internal consistency of their report. An effective report presents a succinctly expressed case for the recommendations made. Recommendations might indicate alternatives open to the decision makers. The readers should be able to track the evidential basis for each recommendation in the various sections of the report.

### 6. Implementing the findings and recommendations

The points made in the second section of this chapter should be borne in mind by middle managers who are delegated to undertake the implementation process. It is essential to check that the intended changes are not being attempted at the same time as some other, equally important initiative. There is ample research evidence to demonstrate that attempts at simultaneous change are unlikely to succeed. The reasons for implementing the findings should be communicated to all members of staff by the headteacher who should also indicate the role to be taken by the middle manager concerned in leading the implementation process. An appropriate time-scale needs to be outlined as well as what will count as success criteria for successful implementation of the recommendations. Appropriate resources will need to be made available as well as any relevant forms of support.

### 7. Monitoring the changes

Monitoring is regarded here as the constructive means of ensuring that the intended changes are occurring. The methods used will vary according to the kind of changes which are envisaged and the level of change which is being sought. Strategies for effective monitoring are outlined in depth in Chapter 4.

# FINANCE AND RESOURCE MANAGEMENT

The TTA Standards state that subject leaders are to 'identify appropriate resources for the subject and ensure that they are used efficiently, effectively and safely' (TTA 1998 Section D). This section seeks to assist the subject manager who is involved in the preparation of the school's annual budget and who may therefore have been requested to submit a budget review report.

**Types of budgeting**

There are two basic approaches: incremental budgeting and zero-based budgeting.

*Incremental budgeting*

This is the most common form of budgeting, in which a school uses the previous year's figures for expenditure as the base for the current year plus some percentage added on for inflation, or a percentage reduction across the board, as necessary.

*Zero-based budgeting*

The previous year's figures are not used as the base. A particular area of expenditure is the subject of review, and expenditure has to be argued for before any sum is allocated. Most institutions select at least one or two areas for a zero-based review in each budget cycle.

## Local Management of Schools and the school development plan

LMS has provided a range of new opportunities in primary schools and has implications for headteachers, governors and staff. The school development plan (SDP) provides within a single source a clear statement of the planned intentions set within a framework of a three-year time-scale. Each SDP is the outcome of a planning cycle which synchronizes with the annual budget cycle so that agreed priorities can be resourced. A strategic approach will require the school to engage in:

- *Budgetary review* – which enables the headteacher and governing body to be aware of the school's current financial position.
- *Budgetary forecasting* – which sets the medium-term framework in which financial decisions are to be made.
- *Budgetary implementation* – when financial resources are committed to the agreed priorities for the ensuing financial year.
- *Monitoring and evaluation* – regular monitoring during the year plus evaluation of the cost-benefits associated with particular resources which have been used or acquired.

## Preparing a budgetary review report

Middle managers are likely to be involved in the process of budgetary review and in many schools subject managers are requested to prepare review reports on their particular area which will form the basis of the curriculum element in the overall budgetary review process.

A review report will contain an evaluative summary of existing provision in the area concerned and conclude with a statement of needs for consideration by the budget committee. Where a school has sub-committees of governors who are associated with the various curriculum areas, reference will be made in the course of the review report to any comments made at sub-committee meetings held during the year.

The stages in preparing a budget review report are as follows:

1. Meet with staff to gain information on:
   - existing levels of provision;
   - experiences of using existing resources;
   - areas where learning needs are not being met.
   (Allow time for reflection and invite staff to identify gaps in existing resource provision and submit proposals for consideration at a subsequent meeting.)

2. Meet with staff to:
   - consider proposals;
   - prioritize the proposals. Ask, in relation to each proposal, 'What would be the effects of not adopting this proposal?'
   - cost the proposals;
   - cost any training needs which may be associated with the proposals.

3. Prepare the review report:
- circulate copies to staff for their comment;
- amend as necessary;
- submit the review report on the agreed date.

4. Assuming that the bid has been successful:
- acquire the resources;
- induct staff into the use of the resources;
- deploy the resources;
- monitor the resources in use;
- determine 'shelf life'.

### An example of a review report prepared by a subject manager for science and technology

This report was prepared by Ms Brownlow (subject manager for science and technology) working in consultation with Mr Renny and Mrs Kenny (Coordinators for KS1 and 2)

*Science.*
The current science scheme was drawn up two years ago as a response to the requirements of the National Curriculum and is currently the subject of a post-Dearing review. Some £3,000 has been spent on science materials and equipment over the last two years and staff have made good use of these. The money committed to extra INSET in science last year (£1,000) has proved a sound investment. As staff have become confident in the teaching of science, they have suggested additions which might strengthen their work still further. Their proposals were discussed and prioritized at a meeting held on the 2nd of March. The prioritized list is given below:

PRIORITY 'A':
- £ 300   for duplicate materials relating to environmental science. These are needed if demands on use are to be met.
- £ 200   for three coldframes for use in connection with KS1 unit, 'Green plants as organisms'.
- £ 350   for equipment needed to support the teaching of 'Forces and Motion' at KS2.

The effect of not meeting the above priority would be to handicap the school in meeting the requirements of the National Curriculum. Their acquisition would not occur any additional costs relating to INSET, etc.

PRIORITY 'B':
- £ 200   to support the school's entry into the local Science Fair to be held in the Summer term.

*Technology.*
In technology the situation is not so positive. At the meeting with staff the following points were brought to my attention: we have too few computers for control technology to be a reality in many of our classrooms. Switching computers between rooms has helped, but it has caused a great deal of disruption to members of staff who use computers for a wide range of other purposes with their pupils. Three members of staff wish to attend a local course on 'Technology in the Primary School' which will be mounted in the Summer term at the teachers' centre. It was felt that we need to develop more expertise on the staff in the area of technology. Not to do so would lead to a shortfall in meeting National Curriculum requirements.

PRIORITY 'A':
- £1,000   supply cover and tutor fees for three members of staff to attend the five-day (five single days interspersed with school-based work) course on 'Technology in the Primary School'.
- £500   contingency sum for expenditure on follow-up to the above course.

PRIORITY 'B':
- £ 300   three sets of micro-control units for use with existing computers.

## Evaluating curriculum materials

Given the spiralling cost of teaching and learning resources it is important to analyse such materials in order to make an informed decision on whether to adopt them. *Caveat emptor* ('let the buyer beware') is a useful maxim for the middle manager to bear in mind. Burrell (1991) has produced a list of criteria which subject managers might find helpful when making the decision to adopt curriculum materials. The potential adopter is asked to look through the materials and then evaluate their effectiveness and appropriateness in terms of the following criteria:

1. Cost.
2. Durability.
3. Appearance/attractiveness.
4. Readability/language.
5. Visual impact.
6. Bias/stereotyping: e.g., how do the materials deal with and present equal opportunity issues?
7. Appropriateness:
   What pupils and educational context are the materials intended for?
   Are they suited to the levels of understanding/reading abilities of the pupils for whom they are intended?
8. Difficulty:
   Do they stretch without mystifying pupils?
   Are they differentiated and capable of being used with a group
   of mixed/wide ability ranges?
9. Capability/likelihood of the materials being completed and/or leading to some degree of success by all the pupils.
10. Interest level.
11. Relevance.
12. Degree of stimulation, e.g.
    Are they likely to lead to further work/research?
    Are they likely to encourage thought, initiative and judgement?
    Are they likely to encourage activities other than writing
    (discussion, visual presentations, experiments, etc.)?
13. Clarity of the aims/objectives of the materials – are these made explicit or left implicit?
14. Relatedness: will they satisfy the objectives decided upon by the teacher for a particular activity?
15. Relationship to other materials, e.g., are the materials testing the same skills, knowledge, etc., or is progression involved?
16. Progression within the materials: the structure and sequence of learning that is implied.
17. Relationship to examinations or other demands/pressures for demonstrable knowledge/skills (e.g., SATS).

18. The range of learning activities contained in the materials.
19. The relationship of content/learning/assessment activities to each other.
20. The nature of the content (knowledge and concepts).
21. The view of the nature of the subject that is implied in the materials, i.e., what are the assumptions about the nature of knowledge/nature of subjects?
22. The view of learning reflected in the materials, e.g., what are pupils intended to do/what skills/knowledge/attitudes are intended to be developed?
23. Assessment – are appropriate tests or other forms of assessment included?
24. Intended use of the materials. What are the implications for the existing curriculum or timetable?
25. What expertise is expected in the teacher if the potential of these materials is to be realized?
26. Are there any INSET/induction implications which will have to be met before the materials are adopted?
27. What threshold level of expertise is expected of pupils?
28. Are the materials susceptible to modification or adaptation?

---

**Activity 24**
**EVALUATING CURRICULUM MATERIALS**

Select a teaching or learning resource which you are considering for adoption within the school This may be a story book, a reading scheme, a set of activity cards, a computer software pack, a pupil reference book, a set of encyclopaedias, an atlas, a poetry anthology, a history pack, etc.
Evaluate the resource using the questions from Burrell's list.

---

# SELF-MANAGEMENT AND THE MANAGEMENT OF TIME

The biggest single demand upon a subject leader is that of time. All that anyone has is 168 hours per week – no more, no less. No one can provide more time – all that can be done is to use the time as effectively as possible. Teaching is an occupation that is seemingly endless in its demands. All teachers will remember the tiring nature of their first school practice and how little, if any, time remained for leisure. The first advice on managing time is probably offered during the first year by a colleague who senses someone else facing the same dilemmas over time that they themselves had faced. Quality teaching and learning cannot be brought about by a tired practitioner who has not achieved the appropriate balance between the requirements of the job and the need for leisure time. If we are serious about raising quality it is essential that we solve this equation in a way which is fair to the pupils we teach, our colleagues and our loved ones. How then might we go about resolving the problem at a time when there is talk of lengthening the teaching week? The suggestions outlined here were identified during programmes with subject leaders whose first remark was almost always 'I haven't got time to take on all that is expected of me as a subject leader'. If time is your problem then give these ideas a try.

**The balance between work and leisure**

It is helpful to start with detailed information on how you currently manage your time. Carry out a simple audit of how you are currently spending your time over a

---

period such as a week or a fortnight. Keep a simple tally of the amounts of time you have spent on different kinds of activity. Use three broad categories and record your findings in a matrix.

- *Work related time* (WRT) such as: preparation for teaching; teaching; marking; attending meetings; talking with parents; giving guidance to and supporting members of staff.
- *Family and leisure time* (FLT): time spent on activities with partners, friends and members of the family.
- *Personal time* (PT): spent consciously relaxing and meeting personal needs: soaking in the bath; window shopping; carrying out relaxation exercises.

An analysis of your record will tell you important things *if you will let it*. Are you managing your time effectively? How do you feel about the balance between the different ways in which you are spending your time? If you are a workaholic stop right there and ask yourself 'Is it worth it?' 'Am I really spending enough time with my family and friends?' Try to ignore such feelings as 'But I couldn't possibly . . . ' and make a firm decision on how much of the week it is proper to spend on work related time. Write the total on stickers and put them on the fridge, the mirror, the door, the car dashboard.

How efficiently do you carry out tasks? Just how long should it take to plan your teaching week, assemble resources, sample pupils' work in a year-group, plan a staff meeting, prepare a talk for parents. Set time targets and stick to them. Even better, if your school is two or more forms of entry, plan *together*, review together, evaluate collectively as described in Chapter 4 under subheadings Sampling, Conversing with Pupils, Pupil Expositions and Sharing Learning Environments. Change to a better balance and you will be surprised how soon you will begin to feel better about yourself and your work. Work hard at achieving this fundamental balance between work and leisure and ask your partner or a working colleague to help you keep on task. You may have to learn to say a polite 'No' to some requests. You will feel much better and less prone to succumb to some form of stress related disorder. Until you have got an appropriate balance you cannot really tackle the problems associated with how you spend your work related time.

## WORK RELATED TIME

It is useful to consider your working day in terms of different kinds of time and then to fit into those categories the most appropriate kinds of task. There is some evidence to support the notion that certain types of task are better (i.e. more efficiently) carried out at different times in the day. There are four types of work related time:

- The length of your *professional day* (PD) (the amount of time that you allocate to school related tasks whether at home, at school or elsewhere).
- The length of your *school site day* (SSD) (the time that you will be working at school and/or available to others on the school premises).
- The length of your *pupil contact day* (PCD) (the times of day that all pupils are in class).
- Your *non-contact time* (NCT) (during the pupil contact day when you are not teaching).

Many subject leaders have very little non-contact time but some schools are trying to improve this situation and setting aside a percentage of the budget to make this possible. It is unlikely that large amounts of time will be given to subject leaders on a regular basis, but some schools are setting aside a pool of time which can be bid for by subject leaders or allocated on an equitable basis.

Many subject teachers on the programmes commented on how they appreciated headteachers who permitted them to undertake professional tasks at home during the school day. This was considered a privilege and the tasks concerned (e.g. planning a scheme of work or writing up the final draft of a policy document) were completed more effectively and in much less time than would otherwise be the case. A 'contract' made by the teacher with the supply teacher meant that pupils got quality time and not merely 'cover'. The freedom from interruption engendered by home-based work was a powerful incentive and most schools had established a set of ground rules that were seldom, if ever, abused.

Consider the above four sub-categories and ask yourself the following questions. Give yourself a score out of 10 to indicate how good the match is between the different kinds of time and the different kinds of task. *How balanced are you?*

1. Am I a lark (preferring to get to school early and undertaking additional tasks before the school day starts), or am I an owl (arriving at school at the agreed time in the morning and staying on at school after the PCD, the self imposed rule being 'I never take school work home with me')?

    The approaches seem to suit some teachers better than others but for some teachers the demands of family life (dropping off children at their schools, looking after an elderly member of the family) are such that they are obliged to have a shorter school site day and make it up by taking work home. In this situation it is important to safeguard leisure and personal time.

2. Do you carefully prioritise your tasks so that you make best use of your non-contact time? A poor match between the type of task and time of day is one of the most common reasons for failing to complete a 'to do' list.

3. How do you spend your lunch time? These are getting shorter in many schools, but where lunch hours are surrendered for the good of the school (recorder groups, netball, choir) some form of time in lieu should be offered.

## SOME 'GOLDEN RULES' TO BEAR IN MIND

- Make a 'to do' list which is realistic and bears in mind the time–task match. If there is anything which is still on your list at the end of the week delete it.
- Most subject leaders on the programmes reported that one of their biggest problems was the unpredictable nature of the demands upon their time, particularly at the beginning or the close of the school day. Teaching is a caring profession and one never knows how important that question by the anxious pupil or that overwrought parent might be, or what it might lead to. Set aside contingency time at the beginning and end of the school day to deal with these. Recognition that this is part of the job is much better than hoping it won't happen. In some schools this fringe time is crucially important in terms of fostering home–school relationships.
- Beware of 'time bandits' who interrupt you when you are engaged in school-based tasks
    - the colleague who drops in for a chat – put a notice on your door stating that you do not wish to be interrupted

- encourage staff to give you reasonable notice when they wish to see you and to give you some idea of what the meeting is about
- set aside time when staff will know that you are available
- keep phone calls to the point – try standing up rather than sitting
- develop polite ways of signalling that your time is limited, or that you must finish a conversation
- where possible get other people to come to you
- keep to the point if you are managing a short meeting (see Chapter 9 on effective meetings)
- try to handle a piece of paper only once – this sounds absurd until you have tried it (look in your briefcase at the end of the week and see how much paper you have been touting about to no avail).

*Try not to be a time bandit on other people's time!*

- Fix deadlines for jobs and keep track of how much time you have spent on particular kinds of task. Ask yourself if you are becoming more efficient in dealing with them.
- Try to undertake the most complex tasks when you are at your 'brightest'.
- Try not to postpone important matters that are unpleasant. To do so will reduce your capacity to work and clutter your thinking. Tasks rarely get more agreeable by being postponed.
- Avoid exaggerated perfectionism (apple polishing) – this will leave you time for more important things.
- As a professional try to set aside a regular reading slot. Personal reading time is usually the first victim to a sudden demand on your time. Is the idea of a staff reading day totally out of the question?
- Remember that quality seldom comes cheap. Remember to submit proposals for improvement at the time of the budget cycle or a good idea may go to waste.

## OVERVIEW

This chapter has focused on a further seven skill areas identified by the TTA in respect of middle managers and subject leaders: leading the team; delegation; managing change; leading an evaluation; finance and resource management; self-management; management of time. Each of these areas will need to be considered when implementing the overall framework outlined in Figure 3.1 in Chapter 3. The final chapter which follows focuses on the equally important aspects of public relations and politics.

# Chapter 9

# Public relations and politics

The socio-political dimension of schools can be represented in the form of a hexagon, as shown in Figure 9.1. In the course of their work, the headteacher and staff are brought into relationship with each of the stakeholders which make up their boundary. These links will be expressed in many different ways, each triadic relationship having its own particular dynamic. There was a time when it was possible for 'heroic leaders' to maintain and resource such linkages, but the degree of change and the range of expectations now held of schools makes this impossible. Relationships are maintained through a widening range of staff who provide relevant information, lead initiatives in response to requirements stemming from different agencies, present accounts of particular aspects of the school, and play a significant role in the formulation of policy. This chapter focuses on governor-school relationships and forms of school-parent partnership. In doing so attention is paid to two of the process skills required of middle managers as they play their part in the maintenance and development of relations across the boundary of the school: representing the school to governors and the effective management of meetings.

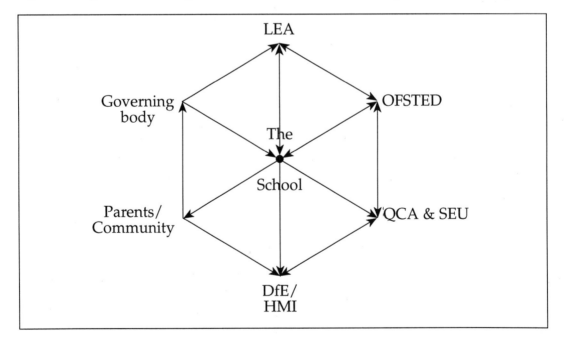

**Figure 9.1**    Triangles of tension and the school

# WORKING WITH GOVERNORS

Subject-managers/coordinators have an important role to play in maintaining and developing school-governor relationships. Governors have a general responsibility for the effective management of the school, acting within the framework set by national legislation and by the policies of the LEA. If they are to discharge this responsibility effectively they need to be kept up to date on the school and its work. Middle managers can do a good deal to inform governors about working practices within the school.

---

### Activity 25
### WORKING WITH GOVERNORS

Read through the list and check how many you have been involved with in your role as a middle manager. Have you:

- gained an appreciation of the role of the governing body by reading through the publication, *School Governors: A guide to the law* (DES, 1989, and updated regularly) which is given to every governor following their appointment? Your headteacher will have a copy.
- Written a guide to teaching and learning in your subject area which can be readily understood by lay members?
- Organized a workshop for governors in which you explained some key aspect of a particular area of the curriculum?
- Designed a key-point observation *aide-mémoire* for governors to use on a guided tour of the school?
- Arranged an adopt-a-class scheme for governors to work with over the course of a school year? Or, alternatively, arranged for two or three governors to visit your classroom as an opportunity to gain experience of the school at work?
- Taken part in the work of the governor sub-committee on the curriculum?
- Explained to governors the key features of a cross-sample of pupils' work in your curriculum area.

---

### Activity 26
### MAKING A PRESENTATION TO THE GOVERNING BODY

Imagine that you have been invited to make a 15-minute presentation to the governing body on the curriculum area or Key Stage with which you are associated. Prepare your notes for the occasion and, having done so, read through the next section on making a presentation.

---

### Making a presentation to governors

- Brainstorm the key ideas associated with your curriculum area or Key Stage.
- Put the ideas in some sort of logical order.
- Select the ideas which you feel will be of particular importance to governors.
- Remember that you have only 15 minutes and that your target is to use all of it to good effect.
- Put the ideas and key points into logical order. You may like to select about five key points, spending about three minutes on each.
- Do not try to cover everything. It isn't possible in the time available. There may have been particular aspects referred to recently in the media which may have caught the attention of governors. If so, these might provide a contemporary flavour to your talk.

- Prepare your introduction, remembering that an effective introduction clearly indicates content and structure to the intended audience (e.g., 'I shall first explain…and go on to outline…Having done so I shall provide some examples…and in conclusion…').
- Decide whether you will have any OHP transparencies, or a handout of some kind, or use a flipchart or a video clip. If you do, keep them simple and don't use too many as this may confuse rather than help.
- Decide on how you will pace the various sections of your talk. What facts, arguments, examples might you cite to help understanding?
- Don't forget to summarize from time to time; you might use a flipchart to record key points as you proceed.
- Have you chosen the most appropriate form of words for your audience?
- Do you plan to refer to notes as you speak? Will these be detailed notes or just an *aide-mémoire* of key points? Or do you intend to memorize the content of your talk?
- Aim for a good first impression; wait until everyone is quiet. Look your audience in the eye, stand still and upright and try to sound and look relaxed.
- Don't make patronizing remarks, even in jest. Speak conversationally. Look for any signs of incomprehension and respond to such signs promptly.
- Watch the time like a hawk, particularly if you have offered the opportunity for them to raise questions in the course of your talk. Let your audience know when the end is in sight.
- Have a clear strategy for concluding your talk. Will you repeat the main points? State the key point in an overall final 'message'? Pose a provocative question? Link it to an activity of some kind?
- Try to leave them wanting more.
- Never, ever, apologise to your audience for lack of speaking ability.

## GETTING THE WORK DONE: EFFECTIVE MEETINGS

As a middle manager you will be called upon to chair meetings in a variety of contexts: staff meetings, meetings for parents or for groups within the community, for non-teaching staff, or cross-school/cluster group meetings associated with your particular subject area. You may find the following helpful in preparing and conducting a meeting when in the chairing role.

### 1. Before the meeting

Ask yourself, 'What is the purpose of the meeting?' Is it a:
- decision-making meeting?
- problem-solving/exploratory meeting?
- fact-finding meeting in which reports are received?
- probing meeting seeking to establish a range of views?
- meeting to disseminate information?
- meeting to evaluate alternative proposals?
- meeting to improve morale/stimulate commitment?
- meeting to brainstorm new ideas?
- progress-report meeting?

If the purpose is that of informing/clarifying, ensure that concise, clear information is made available before the meeting.

If the purpose is that of persuading or making a decision, ensure that the major dimensions and/or alternatives are presented clearly.

If the purpose is that of problem solving, take steps to ensure that the meeting will have a clear definition of the problem and decide on what structures might assist the exploration of ideas and suggestions.

If the purpose is that of decision making, consider how the meeting might best go about identifying alternatives and indicate clearly the criteria by which decisions will be made.

Now ask yourself, 'Is a meeting necessary? Is a meeting the most appropriate form of action?' If your answer is 'Yes', bear these points in mind before the meeting:

- Is the meeting a mixture of the above purposes? If so, what is the best way to order the agenda?
- What items are to be placed on the agenda and what is the origin of these agenda items?
- Have members been invited to submit items for the agenda? Under what terms?
- Decide on the order of the agenda items. Make sure that agenda items clearly indicate the focus of the item and are more than a chairperson's ticklist. Where possible, the authorship of an agenda item should be stated.
- Are there any members who should be asked to speak to specific items? Have they been informed?
- Are there any members whose presence at the meeting is vital if the meeting is to conduct its business effectively?
- Consult with key members in order to decide on the discussion time to be spent on each item and note these on the agenda.
- Bear in mind the purpose(s) of the meeting and structure the meeting accordingly.
- Where is the meeting to be held?
- Who should be asked to attend?
- How long is the meeting to take?
- What information should be sent out beforehand?
- What resources are required? (OHP, flipchart, space for a model, tables for sub-groups, etc.)
- Check if the individuals authorized to take action since the last meeting have done so.
- Send out the agenda and enclosures well beforehand, indicating any key documents which must be read in advance.
- Where possible appoint a process-observer whose job is to evaluate the effectiveness of the meeting.

## 2. During the meeting

Start the meeting punctually, explain the purpose(s) of the present meeting and inform the group how much time will be allowed for discussion of each item.
Chair the meeting firmly but fairly:

- Appoint a minute-taker if this has not been agreed. Do not attempt to act in both roles.

- Identify who will be taking responsibility for different parts of the meeting, if appropriate.
- Gain agreement on the procedures to be adopted in the course of the meeting.
- Try to ensure that all members have an opportunity to contribute.
- If you need to join in an extended debate on a particular item, appoint a temporary chair.
- Control any dominant members and bring in those who may be less assertive.
- Keep the meeting on task; correct any tendencies to drift off the point.
- Be prepared to step in decisively if members become disagreeable during discussion.
- Be prepared to intervene constructively if individuals meander from the point; paraphrase to remind the meeting where it is and highlight to any points which need to be addressed.
- Remind members of the passage of time and press towards a decision where one seems likely.
- Where action is to be taken make sure that the person is named and that you summarize the intended action before passing to another item.
- Remember to thank individuals for their contributions.
- At the end of the meeting, quickly go through all the action points which have been agreed including any which were designated to action by the chair.
- Gain agreement on the date of the next meeting where this is relevant.
- Bring the meeting to a close at the agreed time.

## 3. After the meeting

- Ask yourself how far the purpose(s) of the meeting was achieved.
- Arrange for any summaries, charts, etc. generated during the meeting to be circulated.
- Arrange for information to be passed to staff who were unable to attend.
- Check that the minutes are being written and ask to see them in draft form.
- Check that individuals who undertook to take action are doing as requested.
- Follow up any points which were passed to you under 'Action by the Chair'.

---

### Activity 27
### OBSERVING MEETINGS

One of the most productive ways of improving your chairing skills is to gain feedback on the meetings that you currently chair. If possible, work with a fellow coordinator and take it in turns to observe and give feedback to one another. Alternatively, you could act as observers to another meeting and discuss the insights you have gained in the process. You may find the following checklist of assistance to you:

**A. Evidence of pre-meeting preparation.**
Appropriateness of venue, seating arrangements, etc.
Requisite resources available and accessible.
Was/were the purpose(s) of the meeting made clear?
Were the agenda and papers circulated in advance of the meeting?
Evidence that members had prepared for the meeting.

---

### B. During the meeting

Did the meeting start on time?
Did the meeting keep to the agreed agenda?
How would you describe the pace of the meeting?
How would you characterize the participation rate during particular parts of the meeting?
In terms of the behaviour of the chairperson, to what extent did he/she display any of the following:

clarifying and establishing the purpose(s) of the meeting;
outlining procedures to be adopted in the course of the meeting;
identifying roles to be undertaken during the meeting;
active listening, acknowledging contributions;
giving feedback to contributors;
drawing attention to feelings that were being expressed;
linking points in discussion and pushing the agenda on;
questioning an assumption or a premise;
encouraging reluctant participants;
reconciling different viewpoints;
paraphrasing and summarizing at appropriate points;
presenting a proposal to help the meeting or accepting proposals from others;
clarifying points to assist the understanding of members;
rounding up each item and identifying action points to be taken and by whom.

In terms of the behaviour of members of the meeting, to what extent did you observe any of the following behaviours:

gatekeeping (enabling the contribution of another member);
interrupting speakers;
contributing ideas and suggestions;
volunteering to undertake action;
engaging in *sotto voce* private conversations;
humour;
active listening;
alienation;
aggression rather that assertiveness;
waffling;
synthesizing/resolving disparate viewpoints;
challenges to the authority of the chair;
constructive identification of alternatives;
supporting, confirming, agreeing.

### C. After the meeting

Summarize the key points which arise out of your observations using the following framework:

| | |
|---|---|
| Key factors that lead to an effective meeting | How we can repeat this success at future meetings |
| Factors that hindered the success of the meeting | Ideas for reducing such factors in subsequent meetings |
| Specific chairing skills which helped | Skills which need to be developed by members |

# FORMS OF PARENT-SCHOOL PARTNERSHIP

There is a growing amount of evidence to support the view that schools in which pupils do well are characterized by 'good' home-school relations. Definitions of partnership vary considerably. At one end of the continuum are schools which pay considerable attention to informing parents about what the school is doing and at the other pole are schools pursuing markedly interventionist strategies for involving parents as active partners in the teaching-learning process. Examples of these are to be seen in the many home-school projects and initiatives mounted in a wide range of

LEAs. It is a sad fact that many such initiatives have not survived the 'cuts culture' of recent years.

Pugh (1989) refers to partnership in terms of 'a working relationship which is characterised by: a shared sense of purpose; mutual respect, and a willingness to negotiate. It implies a sharing of information, responsibility, skills, decision making and accountability'. Mary Drummond, (North of England Conference, 1991) stressed communication and the link between words and actions. In her view partnership is concerned with 'doing things, not talking about doing things; the need for teachers and parents to talk to each other, and more importantly to be able to disagree; and for each of them to take responsibility for what each does, both singly and together'. Bastiani (in Munn, 1993), reviewing concepts of partnership, suggests that they involve:

a sharing of power, responsibility and ownership, though not necessarily equally;
a degree of mutuality, which begins with the process of listening to each other and incorporates responsive dialogue and 'give and take' on both sides;
shared aims and goals, based on common ground but which also acknowledge important differences;
a commitment to joint action, in which parents, pupils and professionals work together to get things done.

Hegarty (in Munn, 1993), has expressed reservations about the concept of partnership as it is commonly enacted, pointing out that 'partnership may be an agreeable concept, redolent with egalitarian overtones but the warm glow of right thinking should not be confused with dispassionate action carefully designed to achieve significant targets'. In his view, instead of partnership-type activities we should adopt a functional approach which asks: What activities exist? What purposes do they serve? How do the different aspects relate to each other and to the overall goals of schooling? How do they relate to parents' wishes and needs?

It is likely that coordinators will play a key role in partnership initiatives within their school. Hegarty's questions are useful pointers to bear in mind, particularly in situations where one party or the other has seemingly failed to meet expectations. To lessen this likelihood, some schools insist on parents 'contracting' with staff in pursuit of goals agreed between teachers and parents.

In 'strong' versions of partnership the policy on parent-school partnership is likely to be complementary to the school's policy for teaching and learning and in similar vein should have accompanying programmes of action which are worked towards by staff in a range of different ways. Some schools have abandoned the more traditional forms of communication such as whole-school parents evenings or whole-school curriculum workshops aimed at informing parents about the curriculum-in-action in the various subjects. Instead, individual teachers call regular meetings for the parents of children in their class. At these meetings the emphasis is placed upon the curriculum and plans are outlined for the ensuing half term. Parents are invited to take on the role of active partner in the teaching-learning process. Outcomes are reviewed at subsequent meetings when the work of the next half term unit is explored. Attendance at such action-orientated meetings is usually high; there is a strong sense of ownership particularly where the teachers concerned are prepared to actively listen to the parents and take up ideas and suggestions they may have on ways of involving themselves in the process, either in class or at home. Such an approach requires all members of staff to have a clear understanding of the agreed teaching and learning policy.

## OVERVIEW

This chapter has focused on some of the issues relating to public relations with specific reference to governors and forms of parent-school partnership. Five activities have been presented which it is hoped will assist middle managers in their relationships with governors and parents. Guidance has been offered on preparing a presentation to an audience of governors or parents and activities have been suggested as a means of raising awareness of different forms of parent-school partnership.

# Appendices

The documents contained in the appendices have been produced by schools engaged in implementing initiatives relating to monitoring and evaluation. They are included as examples of working documents which schools are revising and refining as they engage in the process. It is hoped that headteachers and middle managers who are on the same journey might find them helpful in their deliberations.

Appendix 1  Mr K. Parry, Headteacher, Cambell Junior School, Dagenham.
Appendix 2  Mr D. Winters, Headteacher, Heavers Farm Primary School, Croydon, and Ms K. Leng, Assistant Headteacher.
Appendix 3  Mr T. Pratchett, Headteacher, Woodcote Junior School, Croydon, and Ms L. Rowan, Assistant Headteacher.
Appendix 4  Mr J. Clouting, Headteacher, Queen's Inclosure Primary School, Hants.
Appendix 5  A draft policy for teaching and learning.

# Appendix 1

The document below indicates the stance taken towards monitoring the quality of provision in a Junior school which was extending its policy of review and development. It is provided as an example from the field and is reproduced with the kind permission of the Headteacher, Mr K. Parry, B.A.

### Monitoring and evaluating the work of the school
### CAMBELL JUNIOR SCHOOL, DAGENHAM, ESSEX

## INTRODUCTION

This document, which describes procedures for monitoring and evaluating the work of the school, includes definitions of acceptable levels of quality, techniques for gathering information and a schedule of activities covering the school year. It has been compiled following consultation with all staff and is based upon a model recommended by the LEA customised to meet the needs of the school.

Although, ideally, all aspects of the life and work of the school should be subject to monitoring and evaluation, these procedures will be phased in over a number of years, beginning with curriculum policies and programmes. A second category would consist of development policies and programmes which play a key role in institutional development, and thirdly there are the other maintenance policies and programmes which will include the attendance policy or the induction programme for example.

**What is monitoring?**

Monitoring answers the question, 'Are we doing what we say we do?' It is concerned with gathering and organising information on a continuous and systematic basis.

**What is evaluation?**

Evaluation answers the question, 'What is the worth of what we do?' Evaluation describes any activity whereby quality is the subject of systematic study.

# THE MEANING OF QUALITY

We cannot undertake to monitor and evaluate the work of our school without making explicit reference to **quality**, particularly the quality and standard of pupil achievement and the following statements indicate that definitions of quality cannot be separated from the experiences of the users.

- You can be sure of the best quality service with our XYZ.
- They did the repair but it soon broke down.
- They give the kids a good education but they don't tell you what's going on.
- We had a meal alright but the quality was appalling
- I won't go there again, they keep you waiting for ever.
- They give a good service. They do what they say and they are always there when you call.
- They really put themselves out for you.

# DEFINING QUALITY

- Quality consists of meeting stated needs, requirements and standards.
- Quality is achieved through continuous improvement, by prevention not detection.
- Quality is driven by senior management but is an equal responsibility of all staff.
- Quality has to pervade human relationships in the workplace, teams are the most powerful agent for managing quality.

A quality service or product is therefore one that does what it is intended to do and is responsive to the needs of the user. The education provided by the school must match its stated aims and intentions which themselves must reflect the needs and requirements of pupils, parents and the community at large.

# QUALITY CONTROL AND QUALITY ASSURANCE

While the recommended model places a great emphasis upon quality assurance there are elements of both present at different levels of the process.

**Quality control**

- occurs after the process has been completed
- aims to detect and eliminate defective products or services
- is based on checks or inspections to ensure that the education provided has met the required standard.

**Quality assurance**

- ensures that high quality products or services are produced in the first place
- is a commitment by the school to ensure that the education it offers will meet the required standard.

# MONITORING AND EVALUATING CURRICULUM POLICIES AND PROGRAMMES

**Which aspects contribute towards the quality of curriculum provision?**

Three key factors have been identified
- planning

- implementation – teaching and learning
- outcomes – coverage and pupil achievement.

Planning is the process which specifies intentions and strategies, resources, staff and time. Implementation focuses on the classroom and how pupils make progress. Outcomes need to be evaluated to determine both coverage of the curriculum and the standard and quality of pupil achievement.

**Which members of staff are involved in making judgements about the quality of the work and achievement of the pupils?**

The quality assurance model operates at all levels of responsibility and reinforces the cooperative and corporate ethos within the school. The levels of responsibility identified for this school are:
- individual teachers/year teams
- coordinators
- senior management.

**What standards will be specified for an acceptable level of quality?**

It is necessary to define the standards which will be used to identify an acceptable level of quality for each of the key factors noted above – planning, implementation and outcomes. For individual teachers thinking about their own planning a set of quality standards might include:
- the agreed format is used and correctly completed
- learning objectives are indicated and linked to strategies
- relates to schemes of work.

# TECHNIQUES FOR MONITORING AND EVALUATION

In order to gather information to make a valid judgement about quality it will be helpful to consider the use of the following techniques. In many cases all that will be required is for an individual or small group of teachers to check that something has actually been done or taken place. In other cases it may be necessary to gather more information and teachers can match the evaluation technique to the information they feel they need in order to make a valid judgement. (Each of the following methods is then defined.)
1. Systematic checking.
2. Evaluative discussion.
3. Interviews.
4. Diaries.
5. Paired observation.
6. Other forms of observation (by SMT members and coordinators).
7. Taping.
8. Examining the pupils' perspective.
9. Shadowing.
10. Time audit.
11. Curriculum audit.
12. Monitoring assessment results.
13. Samples of pupils' work.
14. Self-reflection.
15. Questionnaire.
16. Reporting.

# A SCHEDULE FOR MONITORING AND EVALUATION

Following a series of staff development sessions involving whole staff and development team activities the attached schedule was produced which includes:

- designated responsibilities for individuals and year teams, coordinators and senior management
- identification of three factors – planning, implementation and outcomes
- definition of standards
- descriptions of techniques for checking.

Three major questions remain to be answered:

## When are these activities to be undertaken?

A time-scale has been added to the schedule which clearly indicates the continuous nature of the whole process but which also identifies key times during the year when particular activities should be taking place. At the same time it gives a clear indication that we cannot attempt to implement the whole process at once. This, of course, prompts the second question.

## Where do we begin?

If the process is to have any impact upon the quality of education we offer then it must be manageable within the time constraints which already exist.

The focus initially will be upon coordinators' responsibilities in relation to outcomes – the mismatch or match between plans and achievement. There will be no consideration at this time given to the implementations stage, teaching and learning, The school's involvement in the Continuing Review and Development Project from January 1995 will allow for this to be phased in at a later date, possibly during 1995–96.

Focusing through coordinators ensures that all staff have a stake in the process. They go into the process with equal status and similar demands are being made of them. Focusing upon planning ensures that a start is being made in an area where many of the specified activities are already happening, albeit informally.

## What do we actually do?

There is general agreement among coordinators about responsibilities within their own subject area which extend across the key stage. For the first time procedures are being introduced which will enable coordinators to fulfil some of these responsibilities particularly those related to planning and levels of pupil achievement.

Coordinators will be involved in a systematic consideration of their subject over an extended period from November to May, followed by a written report for submission to the headteacher by 28th. May 1995.

## A few suggestions

- Using sheets 1 and 2 of the schedule focus first on planning and identify quality standards to be checked, techniques to be employed and a time-scale for these activities.
- Do the same for outcomes.

- Discuss in development teams the most effective ways of organizing the gathering of information, e.g., about standards across the year-group/KS, about completion of pupil records, about planning sheets and agreed time-scales, and about the other quality standards identified above.
- Prepare a diary for yourself which will prevent the tasks building into an unmanageable burden next May.
- Discuss in development teams the best way to use any INSET sessions (maximum two per term) and non-contact time (limited as you know) which will be allocated to monitoring.

# REPORT WRITING

It is never easy writing a report translating a variety of activities into a written document. For present purposes, a report which presents the required information as briefly but as effectively as possible is essential. Two sides of A4 should be the maximum length. The report should contain the following components and it is recommended that these should form the main headings:

- Summary — what is being evaluated?
- Background — why is it being done?
- Methods — how was it undertaken?
  — what techniques were used?
- Findings — what are the main findings?
- Conclusions and — what conclusions and recommendations can be
  Recommendations drawn from the findings?

**A few more suggestions**

- Using the skeleton of main findings write a first draft – do not worry about anything but getting it on paper. It is often easier to write something, leave it a few days and come back to it.
- Write a second draft, improving readability by keeping language simple, removing unnecessary phrases which do not give information, shortening long, rambling sentences and checking jargon.
- Check the report. This is best done by somebody other than the writer as being too close can obscure errors or inconsistencies. Always get someone else to read the final draft.
- Stick to the rules of confidentiality – the report is intended for the headteacher – it may be necessary for another version to be presented to others. This an area which clearly needs further consultation.
- Be prepared to take feedback. Those affected or involved should have the opportunity to comment.
- The report must be seen as a tool for future development and discussion.
- The report should not include personal comments; as far as possible it should be written objectively in order to ensure the findings are regarded as constructive and authoritative.

November 1994.

# Appendix 2

The document below is provided as an example of a monitoring report produced in a primary school. The Headteacher, David Winters and the Assistant Head, Karen Leng have established monitoring as a regular feature within the school.

**Report of the Maths Coordinator on the monitoring activities carried out in the Autumn term 1994**

## KS 1 VISITS DECEMBER 1994

**Focus**

Is a Maths Area evident within the classroom?
Is the equipment well organized and clearly labelled?

A Maths Area was not always instantly discernible. However, the Maths equipment was in each case located in one place and clearly labelled usually with one colour. It was on the whole well organized. **More could be done to promote a Maths Area in each classroom.**

Is the equipment appropriate for the age/ability?
Is there adequate equipment to fulfil the tasks that may be set?
Is the equipment easily accessible to the children?

All the children questioned had detailed knowledge of where to go and get the equipment. They knew how to use the equipment and they were familiar with the various items. The range is appropriate for the age and ability. The children said that sometimes equipment had to be borrowed but this appeared to be equipment that was not used frequently. As the school grows it may be more appropriate for year groups to have their own equipment rather than one central store.

Are there Maths displays?
Are there good models of work on display?

There were factual Maths displays, e.g. number and shape. In some cases vocabulary work relating to Mathematics was on display together with questions relevant to the number line, and shape displays. There were not many displays of children's work. Where the latter was evident it was linked to work on shape and space. There did not seem to be displays relating to other areas of Maths, such as number, measure or investigative work undertaken by pupils.

## KS 2 VISITS DECEMBER 1994

Is the Maths Area evident within the classroom?
Is the equipment well organized and clearly labelled?

In general on entering the classroom a Maths Area is not at first obvious. However, the Maths equipment is stored in one area of the room and clearly labelled. **A Maths Area should be more evident within the classroom.**

Is the equipment appropriate to the age and ability?
Is there adequate equipment for the tasks which might be set?
Is the equipment easily accessible for the children?

The equipment was deemed appropriate but there may not be adequate supplies of equipment given that pupils said that some had to be borrowed. This sometimes came from the central store and was used for topics. The equipment is easily accessible, everyone I spoke to knew where it was kept and what they would need for certain tasks.

Are there good Maths displays?
Are there good models of work on display?

There were factual aids in some classrooms, e.g., on weight, and short cuts for tables work. At first it was not evident that there were many Maths displays. Some displays that I assumed were artwork related, in fact, to shape and space. There was no indication of the Maths content of this work. Again most displays seemed to involve shape and space. There could be more evidence of number, measure or investigative displays. The work on display was of good quality but it could be more clearly labelled.

The children I spoke to in each class could explain their current task and why they were using/had chosen the equipment. They understood their tasks although their replies varied in depth and complexity. Some could predict outcomes when asked. I saw investigations/problem solving being worked on in some classes and the children could explain their methods. They could also talk to me about work they had completed earlier in the term.

**Differentiation**

In number work and number related tasks and with some measure work differentiation between the groups could be seen in most classes. In shape and space and problem solving there did not seem to be as much differentiation.

There are some overlaps in work from year to year particularly in telling the time where progress seems to be slow. Perhaps more revisiting is required to keep this concept fresh, perhaps during five minute snippets at the end of lessons.

Some aspects of Maths were not evident because either they had not been covered yet, or they had been covered in other areas of the curriculum such as art or P.E. In some cases there was no evidence because work had been sent home.

**General points**

Some work had no title or was just a list of answers. I was not therefore always sure of the content. However it may be difficult to put a title to each piece of work. As the children get older they should be trained to do this and also to date their work. **In general presentation should be improved. Work should be laid out neatly, pages should not be missed and where children mount their own work they should be trained to do so neatly.** Pages should not be stuck together!

Rough work on scrap paper should be kept and mounted in their books as it provides the teacher with insight into their thought processes.

**In problem solving tasks and investigations there should be more of the child's explanation of their work, of the rules they formulated, the patterns they found.**

There was evidence of positive, helpful comments written on work by the teacher which showed interest in the results and appreciation of the child's efforts.

At the staff meeting at which the findings were reported the coordinator was asked the following questions on differentiation:

Is it evident?
In what ways is it evident?
Who is benefiting from it?
    low ability only?
    above average only?

How many differentiated activities were planned for?

Was this considered to be too many?

In response the coordinator stated that it was evident that differentiated activities had been planned for and were being carried out in classrooms. Here examination of teachers' planning records, children's work samples and classroom observation had provided evidence of this. **Generally speaking it was the lower ability children who were benefiting. Insufficient attention was being paid to providing differentiated activities for above average pupils. In this sense class teachers need therefore to extend their repertoire.**

Colleagues were reminded of the widely held view that for effective teaching to take place there needs to be a restriction on the number of activities taking place in the classroom at any one time.

To assist teachers with their planning for differentiation copies of articles from *Special Children* were made available.

# Appendix 3

This is an example of a document produced by a school which sets out its stance towards the area of monitoring, evaluation and review. It is reproduced with the permission of Tony Pratchett, Headteacher, and Linda Rowan, the Assistant Headteacher of Woodcote Junior School, Croydon.

### Monitoring, Evaluation and Review

## INTRODUCTION

In 1994 we began a formal programme to monitor, evaluate and review the quality of teaching and learning within our school, to assist our planning for developments which will improve children's curriculum experience and raise the quality of their achievements. We now need to set out our policy on how this programme will be conducted.

## PURPOSES

To provide:
1. Guidance on the development of monitoring, evaluation and review within our school, so that all involved have a common understanding of the key principles and processes.
2. Guidance for staff who monitor, evaluate and review.
3. Guidance for staff whose work is monitored, evaluated and reviewed.
4. Guidance for recipients of our evaluations and reviews.

## OBJECTIVES

Monitoring, evaluation and review will help us to:
  – assess the effectiveness of teaching and learning;
  – improve our curriculum content;
  – improve the delivery of our curriculum;
  – ascertain whether systems are operating and how efficiently;
  – gain insight and expertise from colleagues and others;

- make improvements and introduce initiatives;
- raise staff confidence and competence;
- inform others (Government, LEA, Inspectors, Governors, Parents and children) of developments and the school's effectiveness;
- shape and determine the School Development Plan.

## DEFINITIONS

Monitor:   to gather information, systematically and objectively, over a period of time in order to answer the question:
DO WE DO WHAT WE SAY THAT WE DO?

Evaluate:   to make a judgement about quality by comparing evidence against defined criteria, in order to answer the questions:
WHAT IS THE WORTH OF WHAT WE DO?
WHAT SHOULD WE DO NEXT?

Review:   To look back over evidence and make a considered judgement about the present situation and the next stage of development in order to answer the questions:
WHAT ARE WE CURRENTLY DOING?
WHAT IS THE NEXT STEP?

Evaluation may take two forms:
Formative evaluation – looks at how things are working and how they can be improved during the development programme.
Summative evaluation – looks at the merit of processes and materials and whether this is reflected in the worth of what was observed, after the development programme has been completed.

## STRUCTURES

All classroom monitoring and evaluation will focus on four key areas of our Teaching and Learning policy:
QUALITY OF LEARNING EXPERIENCES PROVIDED.
QUALITY OF THE ORGANIZATION OF THE LEARNING ENVIRONMENT.
QUALITY OF THE LEARNING STYLES AND STRATEGIES USED.
QUALITY OF THE CHILDREN'S LEARNING AND ACHIEVEMENT.

1. Everyone will be involved at some time: Headteacher, Assistant Headteacher, Curriculum managers, Inspectors, Advisory teachers, governors, parents, children.
2. Our programme of monitoring etc. will be informed by the requirements of the school development plan. It is an on-going process which must be manageable otherwise it will become oppressive and will also affect the programme of teaching and learning.
3. These processes will take place through:
classroom observation and interaction
examination of documentation and records
analysis of assessment information
questionnaire
staff discussion and reflection.
4 All personnel undertaking monitoring etc. will do so in a constructive and supportive way. The process must not be inspectorial.

---

5. Monitoring can call upon a range of evidence:
   inspection reports
   direct observation
   reading of relevant documentation including planning
   results of national LEA and school tests
   pupil self-assessment
   parent comment.
6. Staff involved in monitoring etc. will produce:
   a concise report of each monitoring session, for the Headteacher and for colleagues concerned
   a summative report at the end of their programme of monitoring and may be asked to report verbally at a staff meeting or to a Governor's committee. Summative reports, written or verbal, may identify year-groups but not individual members of staff.
7. We will use the information gained to inform decisions on the improvement of the curriculum and the quality of teaching and learning and to plan the next stage of development.
8. Individual reports will remain confidential at all times between the writer, the recipient and the headteacher.
   Individual and summative reports will be retained by the headteacher for inspection purposes.
   Summative reports may be published to the LEA, Inspectorate, Governors and colleagues.

## RESOURCES

Curriculum managers will need quality release time to undertake monitoring. We have already built this in to our existing curriculum managers' programme.

The Assistant Headteacher's monitoring programme has already been built into her weekly release for management duties.

When required the Headteacher will release the classroom teacher for a thirty minute discussion session with the monitoring colleague soon after the monitoring has taken place.

## CONCLUSION

We have already begun to formally monitor, evaluate and review our work, focusing on Teaching and Learning. We have agreed that for monitoring to be effective and of value to the planning process it should proceed at a manageable pace, focusing on a limited number of clear targets. This policy will be reviewed Summer 1995.

# Appendix 4

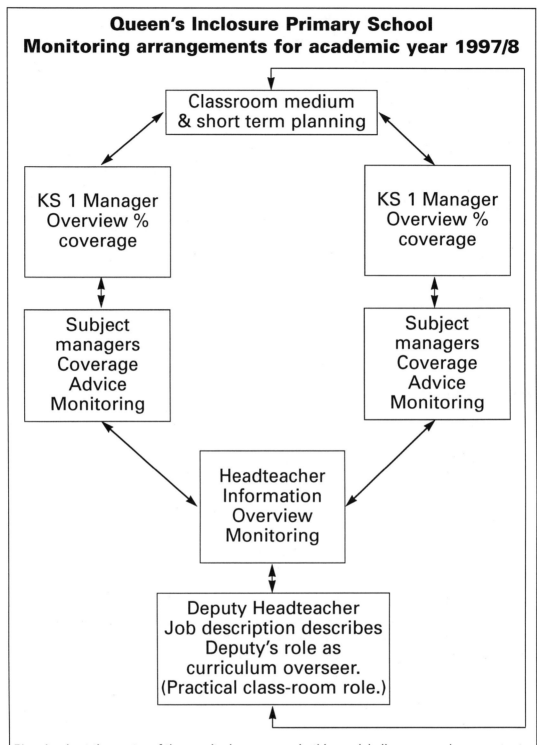

**Queen's Inclosure Primary School
Monitoring arrangements for academic year 1997/8**

Classroom medium & short term planning

KS 1 Manager Overview % coverage

KS 1 Manager Overview % coverage

Subject managers Coverage Advice Monitoring

Subject managers Coverage Advice Monitoring

Headteacher Information Overview Monitoring

Deputy Headteacher Job description describes Deputy's role as curriculum overseer. (Practical class-room role.)

Planning is at the centre of the monitoring process. In this model all managers have access to all teachers' planning. Medium term planning covers work undertaken in units of study. These units may last from two to four weeks or even, on rare occasions, half a term. Short term planning refers to the weekly planning process. Within these plans the learning objectives for the week are recorded. At the end of each week the learning objectives are reviewed and the learning outcomes assessed and recorded.

## MONITORING DELIVERY

**Headteacher**
Monitoring in classrooms against OFSTED criteria. Two days per week intended. In fact 1 to 1.5 days per fortnight have actually been achieved. Improved performance needed for 1997/98.

**Core Subject Managers**
1 – Observation: Continuity and progression.
1 – Planning related to performance.
1 – Report for SMT and all staff.

**Core Subject Managers**
1 – Observation: Continuity and progression.
1 – Planning related to performance.
1 – Report for SMT and all staff.

**Senior Management Team**
For information and action

**All staff**

This model has the advantage of ensuring that monitoring becomes a process of assessing outcomes against agreed policies and not an inspection process relating to teacher performance. The objective is the empowerment of staff and the reduction of anxiety. 'Do as you would be done by.'

Work is sampled by the Senior Management Team once per term. For 1997/8 this will be increased to twice per term. KS Managers monitor learning objectives against learning outcomes to ensure that outcomes are informed by planning within the key stage.

The Deputy Head's role, in partnership with the Headteacher, carries the leading edge in respect of curriculum overview. This is achieved by: attendance at KS meetings once per week. SMT = Headteacher, Deputy Headteacher, KS 1 and KS 2 Managers.

Monitoring is seen as an informative rather than regulatory process. It has developed from the consultative process rather than being imposed. It assists the Headteacher to know, rather than guess what goes on in each class.

*Reproduced with the permission of Mr J. Clouting, Headteacher, Queen's Inclosure Primary School, Hants.*

# Appendix 5

A Draft Policy for Teaching and Learning
Constructed for the Purpose of Critique
**1998**

## 1. INTRODUCTION

This policy statement is the outcome of a series of whole school meetings together with the work undertaken by subgroups of staff who:
- reviewed approaches to teaching and learning and characterised the broad range of ways in which pupils currently engage in the learning process. Thanks are due to all members of staff who cooperated in this essential enquiry.
- reviewed classroom organisation and identified the range of existing practice.
- reviewed current resources for teaching and learning, the location of such resources and major patterns of use.

**1.1** The work of the subgroups has enabled us to initiate a dialogue on teaching and learning, to recognise the complexities of this core process and acknowledge the value which a written policy and accompanying programme of activities would bring.

**1.2** The management of effective teaching and learning is not a simple matter and requires a good deal of sensitivity and careful planning. It is hoped that this document provides a clear outline of our shared intentions as well as focusing on particular aspects which merit sustained attention and support.

## 2. AIMS

- To establish an agreed range of practice in respect of teaching and learning.
- To enable staff to identify aspects of practice which they wish to develop and in which they would welcome support.
- To improve the quality of learning experiences offered to pupils.
- To provide an agreed focus for monitoring the curriculum-in-action.

## 3. NEEDS

The policy seeks to:
- meet the needs of pupils more effectively by offering approaches to teaching and learning and the usage of resources which are consistent across the school.
- meet the needs of staff by offering developmental opportunities aimed at the extension of teaching repertoires.
- meet the need to retain the best features of educational practice when seeking to implement the National Curriculum.

# 4. KEY CHARACTERISTICS OF TEACHING AND LEARNING

(NOTE THAT THE LIST GIVEN BELOW ARE EXAMPLES AND SHOULD NOT BE REGARDED AS DEFINITIVE)

When referring to programmes of study, attainment targets and agreed schemes of work, staff are asked to plan their work so as to maximise the characteristics of teaching and learning we have agreed upon:

## 4.1 The Learning Environment

**The learning environment should be organised:**
- to facilitate regular and sequential opportunities for pupils to develop their ideas through independent enquiry.
- to enable pupils to take increasing responsibility for the organisation and care of learning resources.
- so that available space and learning resources are used to best advantage.
- to ensure that resources for learning are effectively stored and accessible.
- so that learners take increasing responsibility for classroom display and care of the learning environment.
- so that pupils can implement agreed ground rules to support effective groupwork.
- to enable pupils to use I.T. as an aid to learning.

## 4.2 Pupils' Learning

**Pupils' learning should be characterised such as to:**
- enable them to have first hand experience and engage in investigative work.
- enable them to communicate their findings in a variety of ways.
- engage in planned and sequential opportunities to work individually and as a member of a cooperative group.
- meet the challenge of planning and participating in collaborative projects.
- acquire an appreciation of the features of effective groupwork.
- enable them to make choices and play an increasing role in planning and organising their learning.
- produce work for a variety of audiences.
- gain access to the key concepts and modes of enquiry associated with the different areas of the curriculum.
- to practise and apply newly acquired skills and knowledge.
- select learning materials and tools appropriate to the work at hand.
- use modern technology as an aid to learning.
- sequentially acquire basic study skills.
- constructively work under pressure of time.

## 4.3 The teacher

**as constructor and implementer of the curriculum should:**
- value every pupil irrespective of ability, race gender, age or achievement.
- be aware of the model of learning they present to pupils.
- engage in well timed interventions to promote the quality of learning experiences they offer to pupils.

- be clear on the skills, knowledge, concepts and attitudes which are the goals of the learning process.
- deploy effective higher-order questioning techniques.
- systematically engage in focused teaching.
- design challenging and differentiated learning tasks.
- engage pupils in effective collaborative groupwork.
- plan effectively, monitor the effectiveness of the planned activities and maintain effective records on their plans and outcomes.
- distribute their time equably between pupils.
- devise assessment strategies related to agreed criteria and maintain effective records of achievement.
- value and promote partnership between home and school.
- form positive relationships as part of a team.
- value the monitoring process and the opportunities which this provides for dialogue.

## 5. EVALUATION AND REVIEW

This policy and current programme will become subject to review in the second half of the Summer Term. During this review consideration will be given to:

– the value of the policy and programme to staff.
– how far it has achieved its stated aims.

The deputy head will be responsible for conducting the policy review.

## 6. APPENDICES

The appendices attached to this policy document (paras below) give details of the structures and programme of action that will assist in the process of policy implementation.

## 6.1 STRUCTURE

It has been agreed that:

**6.11** Teaching and Learning will be the sole focus of T/L Meetings which will be held fortnightly. Curriculum coordinators will be expected to work with the deputy head in preparing the agenda for such meetings having consulted with staff on particular issues which have been identified in the monitoring process.

**6.12** Monitoring of the curriculum will be undertaken by a task team of coordinators. They will engage in classroom observations related to aspects of practice identified at T/L meetings. Key Stage coordinators will provide support on matters relating to planning and the design of learning tasks and will also collect samples of work relating to aspects agreed at T/L meetings.

## 7 PROGRAMME OF ACTION

In addition to issues arising from T/L meetings, it was agreed that the following programme be implemented in the Spring and Summer Terms.

### 7.1 Workshops on cooperative groupwork will be designed in which we:

- examine research findings related to such work.
- explore what we mean by cooperative groupwork and establish a working definition.

---

- share our experiences of such work with pupils.
- observe two such classes in action during an INSET day
- identify members of staff who will make visits to schools known to have expertise/experience in this area.

## 7.2 Mutual Observation (MO)

During the formulation of this policy document, some members of staff expressed interest in engaging in mutual classroom observation. This will be arranged by the headteacher with the staff concerned. The purpose of MO is essentially developmental and it was agreed that during the Spring and Summer terms participants will identify ground rules which should underpin this activity.

## 7.3 Classroom Display

It was agreed that at the end of each half term, all staff will visit other classes in turn to identify issues relating to classroom display. In the review it was noted that there was a good deal of variation in standards. Sharing practice in this way should help reduce this.

## 7.4 Relevant Documents

**7.41** *An inventory of learning resources* available to staff.

**7.42** *Bibliography* of texts relating to the curriculum and its development.

**7.43** Curriculum structure and organization.

**7.44** Schemes of work.

# Bibliography

Adair. J. (1986) *Effective Teambuilding*, London: Pan Books.

Alexander, R., Rose, J. and Woodhead, C. (1992) *Curriculum Organisation and Classroom Practice*, London: DES

Argyris, C. and Schon, D. (1974) *Theory in Practice. Increasing professional effectiveness*, London: Jossey-Bass.

Bailey, A.J. (1986) 'Policy making in schools: creating a sense of educational purpose', unpublished mimeo, University of Sussex.

Bailey, A.J. (1992) 'Developing school management', Paper for International Conference, Bilbao.

Barth, R. (1988) 'Improving schools for the 21st century', in Parkay, F. (Ed.) University of Florida

Beeby, C.E. (1987) 'The meaning of evaluation', *Current Issues in Education*, (4).

Bennis, W.G. and Nanus, G. (1985) *Leaders: the strategies for taking charge*, New York: Harper & Row.

Block, P. (1987) *The Empowered Manager*, London: Jossey-Bass.

Burrell, D. (1991) 'Analysing curriculum materials', mimeo, University of Sussex.

CACE (1967) *Children and their Primary Schools*, vol. 1, London: HMSO.

Davies, R. (ed.) *Developing a leadership role in KS1 Curriculum*, London: Falmer Press.

Dearing, R. (1993) *The National Curriculum and its Assessment*, London: School Curriculum and Assessment Authority.

DES (1975) *A Language for Life*, London: HMSO.

DES (1978) *Primary Education in England. A survey by HMI*, London: HMSO.

DES (1985) *The Curriculum from 5 to 16. Curriculum matters No.2*, London: HMSO.

DfEE (1997a) *Excellence in Schools*, White Paper, Cm 3681, London: HMSO.

DfEE (1997b) *Raising standards for all: the government's legislative plan*, London: HMSO.

Fullan, M. (1991) *The New Meaning of Educational Change*, London: Cassell.

Fullan, M. and Hargreaves, A. (1992) *What's Worth Fighting for in Your School?* Buckingham: Open University Press.

Fullan, M. (1992) *What's Worth Fighting for in Headship?* Buckingham: Open University Press.

Galton, M. (1980) *Inside the Primary Classroom*, London: Routledge and Kegan Paul.

Galton, M. (1995) *Crisis in the Primary Classroom,* London: David Fulton.

Gardiner, J. (1994) (Chairman) *School Teachers' Review Body,* Third Report, London: HMSO.

Handy, C. (1976) *Understanding Organizations,* Harmondsworth: Penguin.

Handy, C. (1984) *Understanding Organizations,* York: Longman.

Hegarty, S. (1993) 'Home–School relations', in Munn, P. (ed.) *Parents and Schools,* London: Routledge

Hersey, P. and Blanchard, K. (1988) *Management of Organizational Behaviour,* New Jersey: Prentice-Hall

Hewton, E. and Jolley, M. (1991) *Making time for staff development,* University of Sussex.

Hirst, P. (1974) *Knowledge and the Curriculum,* London: Routledge & Kegan Paul.

Holly, P. and Southworth, G. (1989) *The Developing School,* London: Falmer Press.

Hopkins, D., Ainscow, M. and West, M. (1994) *School Improvement in an Era of Change,* London: Cassell.

Johnson, D and Johnson, R. (1975) *Learning Together and Alone,* New Jersey: Prentice-Hall.

Kinder, K. and Harland, J. (1991) *The Impact of INSET: the case of primary science,* Windsor: NFER.

Kutnick, P. (1988) *Relationships in the Primary Classroom,* London: Paul Chapman.

Levine, N. (1994) Unpublished mimeo, University of Sussex.

Lewin, K. (1935) *Dynamic Theory of Personality,* New York: McGraw-Hill.

Lortie, D.C. (1975) *Schoolteacher, A Sociological Study,* Chicago: University of Chicago Press.

McCallum, B. and Street, V. (1998) *An evaluation of the 1996–97 Merton Lead Programme 'Perceptions of Headteachers, Deputy Headteachers and Curriculum Co-ordinators',* London University Institute of Education.

MSC (1989) 'Self Development Systems Ltd', in *Management Self Development: A practical manual for managers and trainers,* Sheffield: MSC.

Munn, P. (ed.) (1993) *Parents and Schools,* London: Routledge.

Murgatroyd, S. (1989) 'Kaizen: a school-wide quality improvement', *School Organization,* 9, 12.

National Union of Teachers (1994) *Your Salary,* London: NUT.

OFSTED (1993) *Curriculum Organization and Classroom Practice, a Follow-up Report,* London: DFE Publications Centre.

OFSTED (1994) *Primary matters: A Discussion on Teaching and Learning in Primary Schools,* London: OFSTED Publications Centre.

OFSTED (1997) *Using subject specialists to promote high standards at KS2,* London: OFSTED Publications Centre.

OFSTED (1998) *The Annual Report of Her Majesty's Chief Inspector,* London: OFSTED.

Open University (1980) *Curriculum in Action,* Block 3, Milton Keynes: Open University.

Peters, T. and Austin, N. (1985) *A Passion for Excellence,* London: Collins.

Pugh, G. (1989) 'Parents and professionals in pre-school services', in Wolfendale, S. (ed.) *Parental Involvement: Developing networks,* London: Cassell.

QCA (1998) *Circular. The National Curriculum in Primary Schools,* London: QCA.

Rauch, C.F. and Behling, O. (1984) 'Functionalism', in Hunt, J.G. (ed.) *Leaders and Managers,* New York: Pergamon.

Remnant, K. (1998) 'Target Setting', mimeo, East Sussex County Council.

Rosenholtz, S. (1989) *Teachers' Workplace: The social organization of schools*, London: Longman.

SCAA (1995) *Planning the Curriculum at Key Stages 1 and 2*, London: SCAA Publications.

SCAA (1997, September) *Target setting and benchmarking in schools*, London: SCAA.

SCAA (1998) *Benchmark information for Key Stages 1 & 2*, London: SCAA.

Schein, E.H. (1985) *Organizational Culture and Leadership, a Dynamic View*, San Francisco: Jossey-Bass.

Senge, P.M. (1990) *The Fifth Discipline*, New York: Doubleday/Currency.

Sergiovanni, T.J. (1990) *Value added Leadership – How to get extraordinary performance in schools*, New York: Harcourt, Brace Jovanovich.

Sergiovanni, T. (1984) 'Leadership and organizational culture: new perspectives', in Sergiovanni, T. and Corbally, J. (eds) *Administrative Theory & Practice*, Urbana: University of Illinois Press.

Slavin, R. (1983) *Cooperative Learning*, New York: Longman.

Starrat, R.J. (1990) *The Drama of Schooling*, London: Falmer Press.

TTA (1998) *National Standards For Subject Leaders*, London: TAA.

Ward, H. (1996) *Science Scheme of Work*, Education Department, East Sussex County Council, County Hall, Lewes.

West, N.F. (1991) 'Planned development opportunities', *Management in Education*, 5, 4.

West, N.F. (1992a) *Classroom Observation in the Context of Appraisal*, Harlow: Longman.

West, N.F. (1992b) *Primary Headship, Management and the Pursuit of Excellence*, Harlow: Longman.

West, N.F. and Remnant, K. (1994) *Managing and Sustaining Appraisal in Schools and Colleges*, Harlow: Longman.

Whitaker, P. (1993) *Managing Change in Schools*, Milton Keynes: Open University.

Whitaker, P. (1994) *Practical Communication Skills in Schools*, Harlow: Longman.

*Video*. The following video is available to support workshops in classroom observation in the primary school. The video is comprised of short extracts from lessons with pupils from Year 1 to Year 5. There is no 'voice over' on the video and it is accompanied by an explanatory booklet. 'Studies in Classroom Observation' (Primary) Ref. No. P 113, available from Focus in Education Productions, 29 Speer Road, Thames Ditton, Surrey KT7 OPJ. Price: £40.

# Index